ANNE MARIE'S

FAMILY FAVORITE RECIPES

WITH A

Caribbean Twist

Second Edition

ANNE MARIE HERMAN

AuthorHouse™
1663 Liberty Drive
Bloomington, IN 47403
www.authorhouse.com
Phone: 1 (800) 839-8640

This book is printed on acid-free paper.

ISBN: 978-1-5462-7033-1 (hc)
ISBN: 978-1-5462-7031-7 (sc)
ISBN: 978-1-5462-7032-4 (e)

Print information available on the last page.

Published by AuthorHouse 11/14./2019

authorHOUSE®

ACKNOWLEDGMENT AND APPRECIATION

Author:	Anne Marie Herman, Retired State and University worker
Style and Format:	Aaron Herman
Proof Reader Assistant:	Barb Booth
Proofing/Assembling:	Joseph Herman
Recipe Ideas:	Helena Dolcee, sister in London, Caribbean Black Cake
Cathy Gerald:	Niece, provided Recipe for Eggless Coconut Cake St. Lucia
Estella Walczyk:	Former Co-Worker, Zucchini Pie
Debra Sherer:	Former neighbor provided rice and peas recipe
Consultant:	Valerie Payne, provided Red Velvet cake recipe

iii

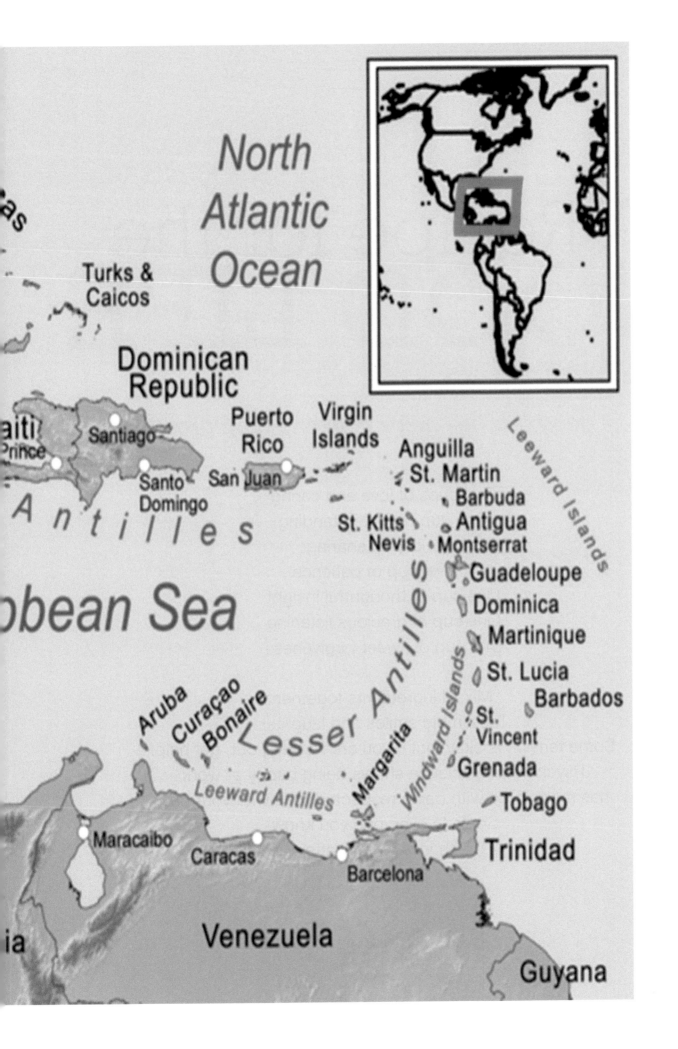

A Recipe for the
GOOD LIFE

A good diet has more than one food group

A heaping cup of Kindness
Two cups of love and caring
One cup of understanding
One cup of sharing
A level cup of patience
One cup of thoughtful insight
One cup of gracious listening
One cup of sweet forgiveness
One cup of obedience
Mix all ingredients together
Toss in big smiles and laughter
Some tension is okay, but if you are freaking out, get help.
Psychological science shows being happy at work
has more to do with being respected than with your pay.
Serve to everyone you know
With love forever after.

PREFACE

Born on the island of St. Lucia, in the Caribbean in a very small house, my father died at the young age of 35 and left six children behind for my mother to care. At the time my father passed away, I was the youngest and only eighteen months old. My father was a farmer who planted vegetable gardens, fruits, and raised domesticated animals such as pigs, goats, sheep, horses, cows and chicken.

I had one sister who left for London, England in the 1960s. When my sister left for London, she left her three young daughters with my mother, which was customary in those days for many in the Caribbean to emigrate to England, Canada or the United States to seek work. My mother and I raised her girls until they were old enough to travel to England and to join their parents.

Growing up in St. Lucia with my mother and siblings, I learned to do what is considered as domestic work in the home and this includes but not limited to cooking, baking, washing, sewing and cleaning. One of my early jobs in the neighborhood was working at a local bakery as a cook. At the bakery, I cooked stews, and baked breads. This bakery had an old brick oven shaped like an igloo with wood and charcoal inside. Wood was burned in the back of the chamber, and evenly created heat throughout the oven. We used a long handle wood spatula to put bread and cakes in and out of the ovens. While at the bakery I made cakes for special occasions such as first communion, confirmation, christening and baptism, and enjoyed decorating the layers as needed. Over the years, I have called on this early experience to bake cookies, bars, pies, and rolls for my children, grandchildren. Now I use a conventional oven instead of the wood and charcoal brick oven but with nostalgia do think of those days on a regular basis.

Cooking became an interest in those early years and I thought it would be a great skill to have as I contemplated emigrating to Canada to work. During those times at the young age of 16 I became a full-time cook, cooking for my brothers Jerome and Robert and their guests. I had moved from the countryside and was now living in the city at one of my brother's home while attending school. On weekends I would return home to visit my mother and while visiting I would also help her with the cooking duties and when returning to the city I would bring meals for my brother as they had become accustomed to it and look forward to my food.

At the age of 24 I married my husband of 50 years. He was a member of the United States military and stationed at Fort Carson in Colorado Springs. I stayed behind in St. Lucia for a short time while my husband reported back to his duty station and then joined him in Colorado Springs. We had two wonderful children who were both raised in Colorado and later moved to Wisconsin.

While living in Colorado, I worked at the Broadmoor Hotel as a machine operator. With the assistance of the Urban League in Colorado Springs, I became a U.S citizen. Later, I attended the El Paso Community College and earned an Associate in Science degree. After obtaining my degree, I took supervised work experience at Operations and Maintenance Service (Project Headquarters for the Air Force) in the Purchasing Department. I also completed additional work-study at the Dean of Instructions Office at the El Paso Community College. After my family and I came to Madison, I was employed at Rayovac Corporation as a transcriptionist for 10 years. After leaving Rayovac, I worked for the State of Wisconsin, and the University of Wisconsin for a combined 26 years. While working for the State, I took evening classes at the Madison Area Technical College and earned a Certificate in Human Resources. During the time that I worked for the State, I was a Program Assistant/Office Manager and was a Site Manager/Financial Specialist at the U.W. In 2010, just prior to the collective bargaining debate at the University of Wisconsin, I retired.

I also worked as a state proctor at the U.W, once a month, I gave State Exams for 19 years at different buildings, checking in applicants, counted exams, give instructions, hand out booklets, recheck applications and finished exams, and recount exams. If we were ever short of exams, then we matched the exams with applicant names. In addition, I have been volunteering at Wisconsin Public Television for 16 years doing various duties.

When I arrived in Madison in 1974 one could not find Caribbean foods in the local grocery stores but over the years that has changed significantly. Chicago and Milwaukee were the closest areas where one could find a minimal supply of Caribbean produce or restaurant with Caribbean influence.

As I am now retired, I have embarked on this project of creating a cookbook, primarily to honor my mother and brothers who I have lost over the years and also to share my experiences in the kitchen with those I love.

TABLE OF CONTENTS

Breads

Cakes

xi

Drinks

Main Dishes

Meat and Poultry

Pies, Tarts, Pastries, Sandwiches and Foldovers

Punch

Salads

Seafood

Side Dishes

Soups

Vegetables

Bring your kids' math lessons into the kitchen

Getting your kids into the kitchen isn't just a way to spend more time with them. It's also a brilliant way to add in a math lesson or two! Help your kids learn measurements in a fun, interactive way with these easy calculations.

Get started with measuring tools from

Anne Marie's Kitchen

2 quarts	= ½ gallon
4 cups	= 1 quart
2 cups	= 1 pint
2 sticks of butter	= 1 cup
1 stick of butter	= ½ cup
3 teaspoons	= 1 tablespoon
4 tablespoons	= ¼ cup
16 tablespoons	= 1 cup

Common
Substitutions

If you don't have:	Use:
1 c. cake flour	1 c. minus 2 T. all-purpose flour
1 T. cornstarch (for thickening)	2 T. all-purpose flour
1 tsp. baking powder	½ tsp. cream of tartar plus ¼ tsp. baking soda
1 pkg. active dry yeast	1 cake compressed yeast
1 c. sugar	1 c brown sugar or 2 c. sifted powdered sugar
¼ c. fine dry bread crumbs	¾ c. soft bread crumbs or ¼ c. cracker crumbs
1 c. honey	1 ¼ c. sugar plus ¼ c. water, heated to dissolve
1 c. corn syrup	1 c. sugar plus ¼ c. water, heated to dissolve
1 sq. (1 oz.) unsweetened chocolate	3 T unsweetened cocoa powder plus 1 T butter
1 c. whipping cream, whipped	2 c. whipped dessert topping
1 c. buttermilk	1 T. lemon juice or vinegar plus enough whole milk to make 1 c. let stand 5 minutes before using
1 c. whole milk	½ c. evaporated milk plus ½ c. water
1 c. light cream	1 T. melted butter plus enough milk to make 1 c.
1 c. tomato sauce	1/3 c. tomato paste plus ½ c. water
1 c. tomato juice	½ c. tomato sauce plus ½ c. water
1 sm onion chopped (1/3 c.)	1 tsp. onion powder or 1 T. dried minced onion
1 tsp dry mustard (in cooked mixtures)	1 T prepared mustard
1 tsp. dry herbs	1 T fresh herbs

Roasting Chart

Meats	Weight	Time	Temp.	Pasta	Cook Time
Poultry				Angel Hair	1 – 2 min.
Chicken (whole)	3 – 4 lbs.	1 ¼ - 1 ½ hrs.	350°	Cannelloni	7 – 9 min,
	5 – 7 lbs.	2 – 2 ¼ hrs.	350°	Fettuccine	6 – 8 min.
Duck (domesticated)	4 – 5 lbs.	1 ¼ - 1 ¾ hrs.	375°	Lasagna	10 – 12 min.
Turkey (unstuffed)	12 – 18 lbs.	3 – 4 ¼ hrs	325°	Linguine	6 – 8 min.
	19 – 24 lbs.	4 ¼ - 5 hrs.	325°	Macaroni	8 – 10 min.
Pork				Manicotti	7 – 9 min.
Ham, fully cooked	7 – 8 lbs.	18 – 25 min./lb.	325°	Pappardelle	6 - 8 min
(bone in)	14 – 16 lbs.	15 – 18 min./lb.	325°	Ravioli	7 – 9 min.
Pork loin roast	2 – 5 lbs.	20 – 25 min./lb.	350°	Rigatoni	10 – 12 min.
Pork ribs	2 – 4 lbs.	1 ½ - 2 hrs.	350°	Rotelle	8 – 10 min.
Beef				Rotini	8 – 10 min.
Beef, rib roast	4 – 8 lbs.	27 – 35 min./lb.	325°	Spaghetti	10 – 12 min.
(bone in)					
Eye round roast	2 – 3 lbs.	20 – 22 min./lb	325°	Tortellini	10 – 12 min.
Tenderloin (whole)	4 – 6 lbs.	45 – 60 min.	425°	Vermicelli	4 - 6 in.
Lamb				Ziti	10 – 12 min.
Lamb (leg, bone in)	5 – 9 lbs.	20 – 30 min./lb.	325°		

Time is based on meat at room temperature before roasting. Time may vary 1-2 minutes
Test doneness at shortest time. Test doneness at shortest time

Commonly Used Measurements and Equivalents

1/2 teaspoon	= 30 drops
1 teaspoon	= 1/3 tablespoon or 60 drops
3 teaspoons	= 1 tablespoon or 1/2 fluid ounce
1/2 tablespoon	= 1 1/2 teaspoons
1 tablespoon	= 3 teaspoons or 1/2 fluid ounce
2 tablespoons	= 1/8 cup or 1 fluid ounce
3 tablespoons	= 1 1/2 fluid ounce or 1 jigger
4 tablespoons	= 1/4 cup or 2 fluid ounces
5 1/3 tablespoons	= 1/3 cup or 5 tablespoons + 1 teaspoon
8 tablespoons	= 1/2 cup or 4 fluid ounces
10 2/3 tablespoons	= 2/3 cup or 10 tablespoons + 2 teaspoons
12 tablespoons	= 3/4 cup or 6 fluid ounces
16 tablespoons	= 1 cup or 8 fluid ounces or 1/2 pint
1/8 cup	= 2 tablespoons or 1 fluid ounce

Favorite Recipes
From My Cookbook

Recipe Name	Page Number

How to Soften Rock Hard White Sugar from supermarket

Sugar comes from plants, or sugarcane, which is a type of grass.

White sugar, also known as granulated sugar, is the most common type of sugar available. It is white and is in the form of granules. When white sugar is packaged, it is placed into bags that prevent the sugar from coming into contact with water and moisture. White sugar has an unlimited shelf life, but when exposed to moisture, it will harden.

Instructions on Things you need

- Plastic food storage bag, large
- Meat tenderising hammer
- Food processor

1. Place the sugar into a heavy duty plastic food storage bag. Seal the bag.
2. Use the flat side of a meat tenderising hammer or a rolling pin and pound the bag until the pieces are broken into chunks.
3. Place the chunks of sugar into the bowl of a food processor. Turn the food processor to pulse for a few seconds at a time until the sugar is unclumped and appears back to its original condition.
4. Pour the sugar into an airtight container. Keep sealed until ready to use.
5. Do not overprocess the sugar in the food processor or it will turn to icing sugar.

Otherwise, placing a slice of bread on top of the sugar in its container will work, but it will take a while.

Or place a couple slices of an apple over the hard rock sugar and let it sit for a while and then go back and recheck it if the sugar breaks off.

Method to soften hard brown sugar

I placed a slice of an apple inside a bag of brown sugar (kept in the fridge) and that kept it nice and moist. I heard it from my former neighbor who now lives in Minnesota.

What do you do when you pull out the bag of brown sugar and it's a perfectly formed, rock-hard, square-edged brick? This doesn't happen often to us (we use a lot of brown sugar), but it did the other day. So we read some home remedies and found one that worked on the spot.

Some Ways To Soften Hard Brown Sugar

It includes some ideas we've heard before, like putting a slice of bread or some apple slices on top of the sugar, sealing it up, and letting it sit for a day or two. That's all fine and good if you have a day or two. We needed our sugar right away.

If you don't use brown sugar regularly and encounter this problem often, consider keeping this instruction for future reference.

Marketplace

Many of the ingredients included in Anne Marie's Family Favorite Recipes Cookbook can be found on related searches for Caribbean foods in Madison, Wisconsin at local grocery stores, restaurants and supermarkets. It is a good idea to check out local ethnic markets, such as Asian markets, East Indian, Middle Eastern, Latin, and Caribbean markets for exotic fruits, vegetables, and spices. Here is a list of local markets where some of the ingredients can be found.

Jamerica Restaurant 1236 Williamson Street Madison, WI 53703 608-251-6234	David's Jamican Cuisine 5734 Monona Drive Monona, WI 53716 608-222-8109
Asian Midway Foods 301 S Park St, Madison, WI 53713 (608) 255-5864	Metcalfe's 726 N Midvale Blvd, Madison, WI 53705 (608) 229-1970
Trader Joe's 1810 Monroe St, Madison, WI 53711 (608) 257-1916	Jenifer Street Market Jenifer St, Madison, WI (608) 244-6646 2038
Tropical Cuizine 15 N Broom St Madison, WI 53703 (608) 250-1700	Jolly Bob's 1210 Williamson St Madison, WI 53703 (608) 251-3902
India House 709 S Gammon Rd, Madison, WI (608) 268-0240	Azacatecana 419 Commercial Ave Madison, WI (608) 240-0778
Willy Street Grocery Co-Op 1221 Williamson St, Madison, WI 53703 (608) 237-1201	Swagat Indian Grocery 6717 Odana Rd, Madison, WI (608) 831-4642

African Market 805 S Gammon Road #A Madison, WI 53719 (608) 441-0276	Capitol Centre Market 111 Broom St, Madison, WI 53703 (608) 255-2616
Metcalf Food Center 2502 Shopko Dr, Madison, WI 53704 (608) 243-1000	Woodman's Food Market, West 711 S Gammon Rd, Madison WI 53719 (608) 274-8944
Whole Foods Market 3313 University Ave, Madison 53705 (608) 233-9566	Hy-Vee 3801 E. Washington Ave Madison, WI 53704 (608) 249-5904
Fraboni's 822 Regent St, Madison, WI 53715 (608) 222-6632	Triangle Market 302 State St, Madison, WI 53703 (608) 255-2116
Stop and Shop 501 State St, Madison, WI 53703 (608) 256-9934	7-11 Mart 1401 Regent Madison, WI 53711 (608) 257-8888
Pick and Save 1312 S Park St Madison, WI 53715 (608) 257-3748	Pick and Save 3650 University Ave Madison, WI 53705 (608) 231-6935
Pick and Save 261 Junction Road Madison, WI 53717 (608) 829-2020	Seafood Center 712 S Whitney Way Madison, WI 53711 (608) 274-5255
Wisconsin Grocers Association 1 S. Pinckney St #300 Madison, WI 53703 (608) 244-7150	Metcalfs West 7455 Mineral Point Road Madison, WI 53717
LA Hispana Grocery 4512 E Washington Ave #3 Madison, WI (608) 271-1648	

Appetizers

Avocado Dip

Ingredients

2 avocados
1-2 sprig onions
Juice of half lime

Method

Cut the avocados in half, and remove the seed and scoop out the flesh. Chop the sprig onions finely. Put the avocados and the limejuice in a blender or food processor and blend until smooth. Stir the chopped sprig onions into the avocado mixture.

Serves 4

Serve this dip with plantain chips or fresh raw vegetables, celery, cauliflower, carrots, cucumber, peppers sliced lengthways into sticks or divided into florets.

Beef Patties

Ingredients

1 pound lean ground beef; 1 tablespoon paprika;

1 tablespoon minced garlic; 1 teaspoon ground black pepper;

1 fresh hot pepper minced; 2 teaspoon seasoned salt;

1 teaspoon dried thyme; 3 large onions, finely chopped;

1 cup celery, finely chopped; 2 tablespoons soy sauce;

½ cup plain breadcrumbs; 3 scallions, finely chopped;

1 tablespoon flour; ¼ cup red bell pepper, diced;

Pastry Shell: Use any prepared pastry dough or see below

1 egg yolk, slightly beaten

Method

Combine ground beef with paprika in a large saucepan over medium heat, and break it up by stirring with a spoon until it is browned. Drain off any excess liquid, and add all the remaining ingredients, except the pastry and egg yolk. If meat is very dry, add up to 2 tablespoons water.

Reduce the heat, stir thoroughly, and simmer for 5 minutes. Remove from the heat and cool at room temperature.

On a floured board, roll out the pastry dough as thinly as possible about 1/8 inch thick. Stamp out circles of dough, about 5 inches in diameter, and place 1 heaping tablespoon of the cooled beef mixture in the center of each. Moisten the edges of the pastry circles with water and fold the dough over to form a crescent. Crimp the edges together with a fork to seal the pastry and brush the top with the beaten egg yolk. Place on ungreased baking sheets and bake in a preheated 400 degrees oven for 30 minutes. Serve warm.

Patty Pastry 12 servings

2 cups all purpose flour
1 teaspoon baking powder
½ teaspoon salt
½ cup vegetable shortening
¼ cold water

Sift together flour, baking powder and salt in a bowl. Rub in shortening and water without kneading too much. Mix until the dough has the consistency of bread crumbs and roll into a ball. Lightly dust the dough with flour, wrap in plastic film and refrigerate for at least an hour. When ready to fill, roll out the dough on a floured board as thinly as possible, about 1/8 inch thick. Cut out circles of dough about 5 inches. Fill and bake at 400oF for 30 minutes as directed above.

Bruschetta with Tomato and Basil

. . . .

Ingredients

6 to 7 ripe plum tomatoes (about 1 ½ pounds)

2 cloves garlic minced

1 tablespoon extra virgin olive oil

1 teaspoon balsamic vinegar

6-8 basil leaves, chopped

salt and freshly ground black pepper to taste

1 baguette French bread or similar Italian bread

¼ cup olive oil

Method

1. Prepare the tomatoes first. Parboil or blanche the tomatoes for one minute in boiling water and drain. With a sharp knife, remove the skins of the tomatoes. Once the tomatoes are peeled, cut them in halves or quarters and remove the seeds and juice from their centers. The plum tomato skins are much thicker and there are fewer seeds and less juice.

2. Make sure there is a top rack in place in your oven. Turn the oven to 450 degrees to preheat.

3. Chop up the tomatoes finely. Put tomatoes, garlic, 1 teaspoon extra virgin olive oil, vinegar in a bowl and mix. Add the chopped basil, and salt and pepper to taste.

4. Slice the baguette into ½ inch thick slices. Coat one side of each slice with olive oil using a pastry brush. Place on cooking sheet, with the olive oil side down. Place toast in the top rack of oven for 5 to 6 minutes until the bread is brown. You can also toast on a griddle for 1 minute each side.

5. Align the bread on a serving platter, with olive oil side up. Either place the tomato topping in a separate bowl with a spoon for people to serve themselves or place topping on each slice of bread and serve. If you top each slice with the tomatoes, do it right before serving or the bread may get soggy.

Serves 6-10 as an appetizer. This can also be served for lunch. Serve with cottage cheese on the side.

Bruschetta

. . . .

Ingredients

1 can diced tomato, drained

Or use fresh tomato diced (dipped in boiling water)

2 tablespoons chopped fresh basil

1 tablespoon extra virgin oil

1 teaspoon balsamic vinegar

1 clove garlic finely chopped

16 slices ½ inch thick baguette or 6 oz toasted

Method

1. Heat oven 375°.

2. In a medium bowl mix tomatoes, basil, olive oil, garlic and balsamic vinegar.

3. Place bread slices on ungreased cookie sheet. Drizzle 1 teaspoon oil on each slice of bread and the oil side facing down and bake 5-6 minutes until golden brown.

4. Spoon tomato mixture on toasted slices of bread. Serve immediately.

Coconut Candy

Ingredients

2 cups sugar

½ cup water

2 cups finely grated fresh or dried unsweetened coconut

Method

Line a baking sheet with parchment paper or waxed paper. Lightly oil it.

In a heavy saucepan, over high heat, combine the sugar and water and bring to a boil, stirring occasionally to dissolve the sugar. Cook until it forms syrup, about 10 minutes. Stir in the coconut and continue cooking, stirring constantly, until it registers 234 degrees F (softball stage) on a candy thermometer, or until a small bit dropped into a glass of ice water holds together and is quite soft when pressed between your fingertips. Remove from the heat.

Drop by spoonfuls onto the prepared baking sheet and flatten to make 3-inch rounds. When cool and firm, wrap individually in plastic wrap. Store in an airtight container up to a week. Makes six 3 inch rounds.

Easy Crescent Veggie Pizza

Ingredients

2 cans refrigerated crescent dinner rolls

1 package 8 oz. cream cheese, softened

½ cup sour cream

1 teaspoon dried dill weed

1/8 teaspoon garlic powder

½ cup small fresh broccoli florets

1/3 cup quartered cucumber slices

1 plum (Roma) tomato, seeded, chopped

¼ cup shredded carrots

Method

If using crescent rolls: Unroll both cans of dough; separate dough into 4 long rectangles. In ungreased 15x10x1 inch pan, place dough; press in bottom and up sides to form crust.

Bake in 400 degrees oven for 13 to 17 minutes or until golden brown. Remove from oven. Cool completely, about 30 minutes.

In a small bowl, mix cream cheese, sour cream, dill and garlic powder until smooth. Spread over crust. Top with vegetables. Serve immediately, or cover and refrigerate 1 to 2 hours before serving. Cut into 8 rows by 4 rows.

Eggplant Fritters

Ingredients

2 cups peeled and cubed eggplant

1 tablespoon white vinegar

½ cup water

1 egg, well beaten

1 scallion, finely chopped

1 garlic clove, minced

1 small fresh hot pepper, seeded and minced

1 tablespoon chopped fresh parsley

¼ cup all purpose flour

½ teaspoon baking powder

Salt to taste

Vegetable oil for deep-frying

Method

1. Combine the eggplant in saucepan with the vinegar and water. Cover and cook over low heat until the eggplant is tender, about 20 minutes.

2. Drain and puree in an electric blender or a food processor. Combine the pureed eggplant in a bowl with all the other ingredients, except the oil, and mix until smooth.

3. Heat the oil in a heavy skillet and gently drop the batter in by the tablespoon. Fry until golden brown. Drain on paper towels and serve hot as an appetizer or side dish.

Yield: 18 fritters

Choose to bake or cook these flavorful ground beef meatballs - perfect for dinner.

Flavorful Meatballs

Ingredients

1 pound lean (at least 80%) ground beef

½ cup dry breadcrumbs

¼ cup milk

½ teaspoon salt

½ teaspoon Worcestershire sauce

¼ teaspoon pepper

1 small onion, chopped (1/4 cup)

1 large egg

Method

Heat oven to 400°F. In large bowl, mix all ingredients. Shape mixture into twenty 1 1/2-inch meatballs. Place in ungreased 13x9 inch pan or on rack in broiler pan.

Bake uncovered 20 to 25 minutes or until no longer pink in center and thermometer inserted in center reads 160°F.

Fried Green Plantain

. . . .

Ingredients

3 green plantains

Garlic salt to taste

2 cups water

1 cup vegetable oil for frying

Method

Peel the plantains, and cut off the two ends. Make a slit along the middle and start peeling off sideways. Slice plantains diagonally half an inch thick. Pour two cups water in pan and add garlic salt. Soak sliced plantains in garlic water for 30 minutes. Pour oil in a frying pan. Drain sliced plantain and fry in medium heat until slightly tender.

Remove from frying pan. Use a piece of paper towel to absorb some of the oil. Smash the semi-cooked plantain. Soak again in garlic water for 15 minutes. Drain and fry again in medium heat until golden brown.

In Haiti, St. Lucia, Leeward and Windward Islands, fried plantains are cooked in this way. The result is very delicious.

Fried Ripe Plantain

Ingredients

2 yellow plantains

Oil, for shallow frying

Finely chopped chives, to garnish

Method

1. Using a small sharp knife, trim the tops and tails of each plantain, then cut them in half.

2. Slit the skin along the natural ridges of each piece of plantain, and ease up using the tip of your thumb.

3. Peel away the entire plantain skin and discard. Thinly slice the plantains lengthways.

4. Heat a little oil in a frying pan and fry the plantain slices for 2-3 minutes on each side, until they are golden brown.

5. When the plantains are brown and crisp, drain on kitchen paper towel and serve. Sprinkle with chives.

For the sweetest flavor, these gently fried plantain slices should be made using the ripest plantains available. The darker the skin, the riper the plantains are.

Hot Bakes

Ingredients

1 pound all purpose flour

2 tablespoons sugar

2½ tablespoons baking powder

2 tablespoons of dry yeast

½ teaspoon salt

1 tablespoon butter

¼ cup milk

oil for frying

water

Method

Pour flour into a large bowl add sugar, baking powder, butter and salt. Mix thoroughly and add milk and water. Knead dough until it becomes soft and almost sticky to the touch. If it becomes too sticky, add a little more flour and knead the dough until you can touch it.

When you are done kneading the dough, cover it and allow it to rise for at least half an hour. Get a frying pan, allow it to get hot and then pour oil into it. Cut up dough into small balls and make flat about ½ inches thick.

Place it in your frying pan of hot oil on a medium heat until it has turned golden brown and turn over to the other side for same results.

Plantain Chips

Ingredients

3 Green plantains
Juice of 3 limes
Vegetable Oil for Frying

Method

Peel the plantain, and slice the ends off and cut each plantain in two. Then slice again in four pieces for each half.

Deeply score the skin with a knife cutting right through to the flesh down the length of the plantains.

Slide your fingertip under the skin and peel it away horizontally rather than lengthwise. Slice the plantains diagonally very thinly. Soak the slices in limejuice for 10-20 minutes. Dry thoroughly. Heat the oil in a frying pan and when hot fry the plantain chips until crisp and golden brown. Drain on paper towels, sprinkle with salt and serve as an accompaniment to drinks.

Serves 4

Plantain chips may be eaten as a snack or served with a vegetable dip as an unusual first course.

Roll-Ups

Ingredients

Roast Beef

4 oz. cream cheese, softened

¼ cup minced fresh cilantro

2 to 3 tablespoons minced banana peppers

1 garlic clove, minced

½ pound thinly sliced cooked roast beef

Ham and Turkey

12 oz. cream cheese, softened

½ cup shredded carrot

½ cup shredded zucchini

4 teaspoons dill weed

½ pound thinly sliced full cooked ham

½ pound thinly sliced cooked turkey

Method

In a bowl, combine the cream cheese, cilantro, peppers and garlic. Spread about 2 tablespoons on each slice of beef. Roll up tightly and wrap in plastic wrap.

In another bowl, combine cream cheese, carrot, zucchini and dill. Spread two tablespoons on each slice of ham and turkey. Roll up tightly; wrap in plastic wrap. Refrigerate overnight. Slice into 1-1/2 inch pieces. Makes 6-7 dozen.

Salt Fish Cakes

Ingredients

1 pound salt codfish

2 cups water

2 cups flour

1 onion chopped and diced

1 teaspoon thyme

1 teaspoon garlic

1 teaspoon chives

1 teaspoon cayenne pepper

1 teaspoon black pepper

1 cup vegetable oil for frying

Method

Put the fish in a bowl, cover with warm water and soak for 2 hours or longer, according to the saltiness and hardness of the fish. Drain, rinse, and place in a saucepan with boiling water to cover. Simmer gently, covered, until the fish is tender, about 15 minutes. Drain, remove any bones and skin, and shred fish finely.

Add the seasonings to taste with salt, if needed, and pepper. If the mixture is too loose, stir in a little more flour until it is firm enough to pick up with a spoon.

Heat the oil in a large, heavy frying pan. Spoon the batter in pan and fry the fishcakes, as many at a time as the pan will conveniently hold, until brown on both sides, about 8 minutes. Drain on paper towels and keep warm. Serve hot as a first course. Serve as accompaniment to drinks. Makes about 20 larger fish cakes.

Spinach and Feta Foldovers

· ·

These tasty appetizers take their inspiration from the Greek pastry.

Ingredients

1 package (4 oz.) crumbled feta cheese (1 cup)

1 box (9 oz.) frozen chopped spinach, thawed, squeezed to drain or put in microwave for 4 minutes

1 medium green onion, chopped (3 tablespoons)

½ teaspoon red pepper flakes

1 sprig fresh thyme leaves

1/2 teaspoon finely shredded lemon peel

¼ teaspoon salt

1/8 teaspoon pepper

1 can (16.3 oz.) Homestyle refrigerated buttermilk or original biscuits (8 biscuits)

cucumber-yogurt sauce, if desired

Method

1. Heat oven to 375°F. Spray large cookie sheet with cooking spray.
2. In medium bowl, place feta cheese; break apart large pieces with fork. Add spinach, onions, lemon peel, fresh thyme leaves, red pepper flakes, salt and pepper; mix well.
3. Separate dough into 8 biscuits. Separate each biscuit into 2 layers. Press or roll each to form 3 1/2-inch round. Place about 2 tablespoons spinach mixture on center of each round. Fold dough over filling, pressing firmly to compress filling; firmly press edges of dough with fork to seal. Place on cookie sheet.

4. Bake 12 to 16 minutes or until golden brown. Cool 5 minutes. Serve warm with cucumber-yogurt sauce. Makes 16 appetizers

Success

Edges of dough must be firmly pressed with fork to seal completely during baking.

Cucumber-yogurt sauce is traditional Greek yogurt sauce with cucumber and herbs. Look for them in the refrigerated section of the deli area at your grocery store.

Bars

Almond Coconut Candy Bar

Ingredients

1 cup semisweet chocolate chips

¼ cup butter

½ cup chocolate cookie crumbs

Filling

3 egg whites

1 cup sugar

2 teaspoons vanilla

½ teaspoon almond extract

2½ cups coconut

¾ cup all-purpose flour

36 whole almonds

2 ½ cups shredded unsweetened coconut

Glaze

½ cup semisweet chocolate chips

3 tablespoons butter

Method

Heat oven to 350°F. Line 13x9-inch pan with foil. Spray foil with nonstick cooking spray. In small saucepan, combine 1 cup chocolate chips and ¼ cup butter; melt over low heat, stirring occasionally. Stir in cookie crumbs. Spread mixture evenly in bottom of sprayed foil-lined pan. Refrigerate 15 minutes or until set.

Meanwhile, in large bowl, beat egg whites until soft peaks form. Gradually add sugar, beating until stiff peaks form. Meanwhile, in a large bowl, add vanilla blend well. Stir in shredded coconut and flour until well mixed.

Spread filling evenly over base. Arrange almonds over bars in 6 rows of 6 each.

Bake at 350°F for 20 to 25 minutes or until lightly browned and center is set when lightly touched.

In small saucepan, melt glaze ingredients over low heat, stirring frequently until smooth. Drizzle glaze over bars. Cool at least 4 hours or until set. Cut into bars.

These bars have the almond and coconut flavors of a popular candy bar.

Use semisweet chocolate squares in place of chocolate chips. Use three 1 ounce squares for 1/2 cup of chips. Coarsely chop the squares so the chocolate will melt easily and uniformly.

Cereal Breakfast Bars

Ingredients

3 cups miniature marshmallows

½ cup peanut butter

½ cup nonfat dry milk

¼ cup orange flavored instant breakfast drink

1 cup raisins

4 cups O-shaped puffed oat cereal

Method

1. In a large saucepan, melt butter and marshmallows over low heat, stirring constantly.
2. Stir in peanut butter until melted. Mix in milk and breakfast drink.
3. Remove from heat and fold in raisins, cereal, and stir until evenly coated.
4. With buttered hands, pat evenly into buttered baking pan, 9 X 9 X 2 inches. Cool and cut into bars about 3 X 1 inch.
5. Two bars and a glass of skimmed milk make a nutritious breakfast on the run, furnishing ¼ of the Minimum Daily Requirements.

Chocolate Chip-Popcorn Bars

Ingredients

Crust

1 roll (16.5 ounces) refrigerated chocolate chip cookies

4 Oats and honey crunchy granola bars (2 pouches from 8.9 ounces box), crushed

Topping

3 ½ cups miniature marshmallows

1 bag (3.5 oz) butter flavor microwave popcorn, popped

2/3 cup light corn syrup

¼ cup butter

1 bag (10 ounces) peanut butter chips

1 cup semisweet chocolate chips

Method

1. Heat oven to 350°F. In large bowl, break up cookie dough. Stir in crushed granola bars. Press evenly in bottom of ungreased 13x9 inch pan to form crust.

2. Bake 10 to 15 minutes or until puffed and edges are golden brown. Sprinkle with marshmallows. Bake 1 to 2 minutes longer or until marshmallows begin to puff.

3. Remove and discard unpopped kernels from popped popcorn. In 3-quart saucepan, heat corn syrup, butter and peanut butter chips over medium heat 3 to 4 minutes, stirring frequently, until chips are melted and mixture is smooth. Stir in popcorn (mixture will be thick). Spoon over marshmallows; spread evenly to just barely cover marshmallows. Cool 30 minutes.

4. In small microwavable bowl, microwave chocolate chips on High 1 minute to 1 minute 30 seconds, stirring once halfway through microwaving, until melted. Pour melted chocolate into 1-quart resealable food storage plastic bag. Cut off tiny bottom corner of bag; drizzle chocolate over bars. Refrigerate at least 1 hour before serving. For bars, cut into 6 rows by 6 rows.

Cream Cheese Pumpkin Bars

Ingredients

4 eggs

1 2/3 cup sugar

1 cup oil

1 16 oz. can pumpkin

2 cups flour

2 teaspoons baking powder

2 teaspoons cinnamon

1 teaspoon salt

1 teaspoon baking soda

3 oz. cream cheese, softened

½ cup butter, softened

1 teaspoon almond extract

2 cups powdered sugar

1 teaspoon almond extract

Method

In a mixing bowl, beat together eggs, sugar, oil, and pumpkin until light and fluffy. Stir together flour, baking powder, cinnamon, salt and soda. Add to pumpkin mixture and mix thoroughly.

Spread batter in greased and floured 9 X 13 pan. Bake at 350 degrees oven for about 35 minutes. Remove from oven and allow cooling.

Cream together cream cheese and butter. Stir in almond extract. Add confectioners sugar, a little at a time, beat until smooth. Spread on cooled bars. Cut into squares.

Cream of Cheese Bars

Ingredients

½ cup butter

1¼ cup flour

½ cup rolled oats

¼ teaspoon salt

8 oz. soft cream cheese

1/3 cup sugar

1 egg

2½ teaspoon grated lemon rind

1 teaspoon lemon juice

¼ cup milk

Method

1. Combine first four ingredients and mix until crumbly.
2. Press half in bottom of ungreased square pan.
3. Set other half aside.
4. Combine remaining ingredients. Beat until smooth and creamy.
5. Pour over crust. Top with remaining crumb mixture. Bake at 350° for 35 to 40 minutes.
6. Cool, cut into squares.

Favorite Brownies

· ·

Ingredients

½ cup shortening

2 squares unsweetened chocolate

1½ cup sugar

3 eggs

1cup flour

½ teaspoon baking powder

½ teaspoon salt

1 teaspoon vanilla

½ cup chopped walnuts

Method

1. Melt shortening and chocolate together.
2. Stir eggs into melted mixture.
3. Combine dry ingredients.
4. Stir in walnuts and vanilla.
5. Pour into 9 inch greased pan and bake at 350° for 30 minutes.

Fudgy Fudge Brownies

Ingredients

1 1/4 cup flour

1/4 cup cocoa

1 teaspoon baking powder

1/2 teaspoon salt

3 eggs

2 cup sugar

3/4 cup butter, melted

1 teaspoon vanilla extract

1 cup chopped walnuts

Method

1. Mix together flour, cocoa, baking powder, salt and walnuts. Set aside.
2. In large bowl, combine eggs, sugar, butter and vanilla. Beat with wooden spoon until smooth. Stir in dry ingredients; mix well. Spread batter evenly in greased 13X9 inch pan.
3. Bake in 350°F oven for about 25 minutes. Brownies are ready when edges are just set and center is still soft.

Vanilla Icing:

1/3 cup butter

2 cup confectioners' sugar (icing sugar)

2 tablespoons milk

1/4 teaspoon vanilla extract

Beat ingredients together and spread on top of brownies. Cut into squares.

Layered Bars

Ingredients

1 can (8 oz.) refrigerated dinner rolls
(Seamless dough sheet)

1 cup white vanilla baking chips

1 cup semisweet chocolate chips

1 cup slivered almonds

1 cup cashew halves and pieces

1 can (14 oz.) sweetened condensed milk
(Not evaporated)

Method

1. Heat oven to 375°F (350°F for dark pans). Grease bottom and sides of 13x9-inch pan.

2. If using dinner rolls: Unroll dough into 2 long rectangles. If using dough sheet: Unroll dough. Place in pan; press over bottom and 1/2 inch up sides to form crust. Bake 5 minutes.

3. Remove partially baked crust from oven. Sprinkle vanilla chips, chocolate chips, almonds and cashews evenly over crust. Pour condensed milk evenly over top.

4. Return to oven; bake 20 to 25 minutes longer or until golden brown. Cool 15 minutes. Run knife around sides of pan. Cool 1 hour. Refrigerate about 30 minutes or until chocolate is set.

Lemon Squares

Ingredients

2 cups flour

1 cup butter

½ cup sugar

4 eggs

1½ cup sugar

1 teaspoon baking powder

¼ cup flour

½ teaspoon salt

4 tablespoons lemon juice

Powdered confectioners sugar

Method

Mix together until crumbly, the flour, butter, and sugar. Press into greased 13X9 inch pan. Bake for 20 minutes at 350°F.

In a separate bowl, beat the eggs; add sugar, baking powder, flour, salt, and lemon juice. Beat together and pour gently over baked crust.

Bake 20 minutes longer at 350°F. Do not overbake. It should just be slightly brown. When cool sprinkle with confectioners' sugar. Makes 32 bars.

Mud Hen Bars

Ingredients

½ cup shortening

1 cup white sugar

1 egg and 2 egg yolks

1½ cup flour

1 teaspoon baking powder

¼ tsp salt

1 cup semisweet chocolate chips

1 cup marshmallows

1 cup brown sugar

1 cup chopped peanuts

Method

Preheat oven to 350°

1. Mix ½ cup shortening and 1 cup white sugar.
2. Add 1 whole egg and 2 eggs separated
3. In a separate bowl, sift flour, baking powder and salt together;
4. Combine flour mixture, blending thoroughly.
5. Spread batter in 9 x 13 x 2 inch pan. Sprinkle 1 cup chocolate chips and 1 cup marshmallows over batter.
6. Beat the two egg whites stiff. Fold in 1 cup brown sugar.
7. Spread over batter. Sprinkle with chopped nuts.
8. Bake 350° for 30-40 minutes.
9. Cool then cut into bars. Makes 32 bars.

Orange Cream Dessert Squares

· ·

Ingredients

1 roll (16.5 oz.) refrigerated sugar cookies

2 tablespoons grated orange peel (from 2 large oranges)

2 packages (8 oz. each) cream cheese, softened

¼ cup sugar

½ cup sweet orange marmalade

1 teaspoon orange-flavored liqueur or

1/4 teaspoon orange extract

2 eggs

3 tablespoons whipping (heavy) cream

2 drops orange food color or

(2 drops yellow and 1 drop red food color)

1½ teaspoons butter

½ cup white vanilla baking chips

Method

1. Heat oven to 350°F. Press cookie dough on bottom of ungreased 13x9 inch glass baking dish. Sprinkle evenly with orange peel.

2. In medium bowl, beat cream cheese, sugar, marmalade and liqueur with electric mixer on medium high speed about 1 minute or until well blended.

3. Add eggs; until well blended and mixture is creamy.

4. Spread evenly on crust. Bake 29 to 36 minutes or until crust is golden brown and center is set. Cool 1 hour.

5. In small bowl, microwave whipping cream and food color uncovered on High about 30 seconds or just until boiling.

6. Add butter and baking chips; stir until chips are melted. Spread mixture evenly over bars.

7. Refrigerate about 1 1/2 hours or until chilled and firm. To serve, cut into 6 rows by 4 rows, using thin, sharp knife and wiping blade occasionally.

8. Cover and refrigerate any remaining dessert squares.

Pumpkin Bars With Cream Cheese Frosting

. . . .

Ingredients

2 cup flour

1 1/2 cups sugar

2 teaspoons baking powder

2 teaspoons ground cinnamon

1 teaspoon baking soda

1/4 teaspoon salt

1/4 teaspoon ground cloves

4 eggs, beaten

1 (16 oz.) can pumpkin

1 cup cooking oil

Method

Combine flour, sugar, baking powder, cinnamon, soda, salt and cloves. Stir in eggs, pumpkin and oil until mixed thoroughly. Spread batter into an ungreased 15 x 10 x 1 inch pan.

Bake in a 350-degree oven for 25 to 30 minutes or until toothpick inserted near center comes out clean. Cool on wire rack. Frost with cream cheese frosting.

CREAM CHEESE FROSTING:
2 (3 oz.) packages cream cheese
1/2 cups butter, softened
2 teaspoons vanilla
2 ½ cups powdered sugar

In bowl, mix cream cheese, butter and vanilla until light and fluffy. Gradually add 2 cups powdered sugar; beat well. Gradually add enough remaining powdered sugar to make frosting of spreading consistency.

White Chocolate Berry Bars

. . . .

Ingredients

2 cups milk

½ cup whipping cream

1-4 serving size instant white chocolate pudding mix

5 to 8 drops blue or red food coloring

1cup fresh or frozen blueberries,

Chopped strawberries, or whole raspberries

Method

In a blender combine milk, whipping cream, and pudding mix. Cover and blend until smooth. For blue pops, add 5 to 8 drops blue food coloring. For pink pops, add 5 to 8 drops red food coloring. Cover and blend until combined.

Transfer to a medium bowl. Let stand 5 minutes; stir in fruit.

Pour or spoon mixture into eight to ten 3-ounce paper or plastic drink cups or frozen pop molds. Cover cups with foil; cut a slit in the foil and insert wooden sticks (or cover according to manufacturer directions). Freeze 4 hours or overnight. Makes 8 to 10 (3 ounce) pops.

Breads

Aloha Friendship Bread

. . . .

Ingredients

4 cups unbleached flour

1 1/2 cup sugar

1 teaspoon baking powder

1 teaspoon salt

1½ cup shredded coconut (unsweetened)

1 cup macadamia nuts (chopped walnuts works fine) optional

2 cups canned, crushed pineapple unsweetened in its own juice

3 large eggs beaten

1 cup buttermilk (one) ½ pint size

¼ cup oil

Method

Preheat oven 375ºF degrees and grease two 8½ X 4½ inch or four 5X3 1/2 loaf pans. In a large bowl, thoroughly whisk flour, sugar, baking powder and salt. Stir in coconut and macadamia nuts. In separate bowl combine, pineapple in its own juice, eggs, buttermilk, and oil. Stir into flour mixture until blended. Spoon batter into greased and floured pans. Bake 375º 8 ½ inch loaves 1-1/4 hours and 5 inch loaves 35-40 minutes, until breads are golden brown and spring back to the touch, or they test done with a wooden pick. Cool 10 minutes in pans, then turn out onto wire racks to cool completely before slicing.

Banana Coconut Bread

. . . .

Ingredients

3 very ripe bananas

½ cup shortening or butter

¾ cup sugar

2 eggs

½ teaspoon vanilla extract

1 cup all purpose flour

1 cup whole wheat flour

½ teaspoon salt

1 teaspoon baking powder

1/4 teaspoon freshly grated nutmeg or ground cinnamon

1/3 cup hot water

1 cup unsweetened medium thread dried coconut

Method

Preheat oven to 325°. Grease and flour a 9 X 5 inch loaf pan. Peel the bananas and place in a small bowl. Using a folk, mash until smooth.

In a separate bowl, combine the shortening and sugar and beat with an electric mixer until fluffy. Add the eggs, bananas, vanilla, and beat well.

In another bowl, stir together the flours, salt, baking powder, and nutmeg or ground cinnamon. Beat the flour mixture into the banana mixture alternately with the hot water, beginning and ending with the flour mixture. When fully incorporated, stir in the coconut. Pour into the prepared loaf pan.

Bake until a thin skewer inserted in the center comes out clean or the top bounces back when lightly touched, about 1 hour and 10 minutes. Remove from the oven and transfer to a rack. Let cool at least 15 minutes, then take out of the pan and slice to serve. Store in the refrigerator wrapped in plastic wrap up to 5 days.

Banana Muffin Surprise

Ingredients

½ cup uncooked oats

½ cup milk

1 cup all-purpose flour

¼ cup sugar

2½ teaspoons baking powder

½ teaspoon each soda, salt, and cinnamon

¼ teaspoon nutmeg

¼ cup butter

1 egg, beaten

1 cup mashed bananas

½ cup sunflower seeds

Method

Preheat oven and bake at 425 degree for 15 minutes or until muffins test done. Yield 12 to 14 muffins.

Combine oats and milk in medium bowl. Set aside until milk is absorbed. Mix next 7 ingredients in medium bowl. Add butter, egg, and bananas to oat mixture; mix well. Add to dry ingredients; stir until just mixed. Stir in sunflower seeds. Fill greased 2 ½ inch muffin cups 2/3 full and bake.

Bran Muffins

Ingredients

6 cups bran cereal

4 beaten eggs

1 cup oil

5 cups flour

2 cups boiling water

5 teaspoon baking soda

1 teaspoon salt

1 quart buttermilk

3 cups sugar

Method

Pour boiling water over cereal and let cool for 20 minutes.

Stir in rest of ingredients until blended.

Use double paper cups and fill ½ full. Bake 350°F 30 minutes. Muffin batter stays in the refrigerator for 2 weeks. Makes 5 dozen.

Easy Cheese Bread

Ingredients

2 packets dry yeast
1 11-oz. can cheddar cheese soup
1 packet dry Italian salad dressing mix
3 ½ to 3¾ cup flour

Method

1. Soften yeast in ½ cup warm water in large bowl. Add soup and salad dressing mix. Add flour gradually to make stiff dough, beating well.
2. Knead dough on floured surface for about 5 minutes until smooth and elastic. Place in greased bowl, turning to grease surface. Cover and let rise in warm place for 30 minutes or until doubled in size.
3. Shape dough into four 10-inch loaves. Place on greased cookie sheets cover and let rise for 30 minutes or until doubled in size.
4. Bake at 400 degrees for 30 to 40 minutes. Remove from pans immediately, cool on wire racks.

French Breakfast Puffs

Ingredients

1/3 cup butter, softened

½ cup sugar

1 egg

1 1/2 cups flour

1 1/2 teaspoon baking powder

½ teaspoon salt

¼ teaspoon nutmeg

½ cup milk

Topping:

2 - 4 tablespoons melted butter

¼ cup sugar

½ teaspoon cinnamon

Method

Preheat oven to 350 °F.

Either grease a muffin tin, or put the paper cups into the muffin cups.

I like to make 24 mini muffins, but this recipe is perfect for 12 regular muffins.

Cream the butter, sugar, and eggs, either by hand or with a hand-held mixer.

Combine the dry ingredients and add them to the creamed mixture alternately with the milk.

Fill muffin cups 2/3 full and bake until golden brown, 20 - 25 minutes for the regular muffins, less for the smaller ones.

While still hot either dip the top of the muffin in the melted butter, or brush on the melted butter, then dip the muffin into the mix of cinnamon and sugar.

Fresh Apple Bread

Ingredients

2 cups sifted flour

1 teaspoon baking soda

1 teaspoon baking powder

½ teaspoon salt

1 teaspoon cinnamon

½ cup shortening

1 cup sugar

2 eggs

1½ cup chopped baking apple

½ cup chopped nuts

1 teaspoon vanilla

Method

1. Sift together the flour, baking powder, baking soda, salt and cinnamon.
2. Cream shortening, sugar and eggs; add apples. Stir in flour mixture.
3. Pour batter in greased 9 X 5 X 3 inch bread pan.
4. Sprinkle with a topping mixture of ¼ cup sugar and 1½ teaspoons cinnamon. Bake in a 350° F oven for 1 hour. Turn pan on its side to cool.

Hot Cross Buns

Perfect bread for Good Friday

Ingredients

1 ½ cup boiling water

¼ cup chilled butter, chopped

½ cup sugar

1 teaspoon salt

1 cup evaporated milk

1 teaspoon or (2 packets ½ oz.) active dry yeast

2 large eggs beaten

7 cups flour

1 cup dried currants, optional

1 tablespoon butter, melted

¾ cup confectioner's sugar

Evaporated milk for icing

Method

1. Put chopped butter into large bowl and pour boiling water over it. Stir until the butter is dissolved. Stir in sugar and salt. Stir in 1 cup evaporated milk and let mixture cool to lukewarm. Stir yeast into lukewarm liquid. Mix in eggs and 4 cups of flour. Mix in currants, if desired. Add the remaining flour to make soft dough. Turn dough out onto floured board and knead for 5 minutes. Place dough in greased bowl. Turn dough over so that the top is lightly greased. Cover and let rise in warm, draft free place for 1 hour. Punch down dough and knead for 3 more minutes. Shape dough into 18 buns.

2. Set buns on greased baking sheets and cut a cross on the tops of each bun. Cover and let rise for about 30 minutes or until double in size. Bake at 450 degrees for 10 to 15 minutes.

3. Remove buns from oven and brush with melted butter. Set on rack to cool.

4. Mix confectioner's sugar with enough evaporated milk to make a thick icing. Ice the cross you cut into each bun. Let stand until icing thickens on buns.

Hush Puppies

Ingredients

½ cup corn meal

½ cup flour

1 teaspoon salt

¾ cup milk

1 small onion, diced

1 egg, well beaten

Oil for frying

Method

Mix dry ingredients. Add milk and egg. Mix again and add onion. Mix again. Batter comes out thin. Drop a teaspoon in deep fat or oil and fry till golden brown. When done place on paper towel for 5 to 10 minutes and serve.

Lemony Carrot-Walnut Bread

. . . .

Ingredients

1½ cups bran cereal, crushed

1 can (14.5 oz.) sliced carrots, drained, reserve 1/2 cup of liquid

1 teaspoon grated lemon peel

1/3 cup lemon juice

¼ cup vegetable oil

2 eggs

2 2/3 cups all-purpose flour

¾ cup sugar

2 teaspoons baking powder

2 teaspoons pumpkin pie spice

½ teaspoon baking soda

¼ teaspoon salt

½ cup chopped walnuts

Method

Heat oven to 350°F. Grease bottom only of 9x5 inch loaf pan with shortening or cooking spray. Place cereal in food storage plastic bag; crush with rolling pin (or crush in food processor). Set aside.

In large bowl, drain liquid from the can and mash carrots with fork. With electric mixer on low speed, beat in reserved carrot liquid, lemon peel, lemon juice, oil and eggs until blended.

Beat in flour, sugar, baking powder, pumpkin pie spice, baking soda, and salt until blended. Stir in crushed cereal and walnuts. Spoon batter into pan.

Bake about 1 hour 15 minutes or until toothpick inserted in center comes out clean. Cool 15 minutes; remove from pan to cooling rack. Cool completely for about 1 hour, before slicing.

Savory Bruschetta

Ingredients

¼ cup olive oil

1 clove garlic, minced

1 loaf French bread, cut in half lengthwise

1 8-oz. package cream cheese, softened

3 tablespoons grated Parmesan cheese

2 tablespoons chopped pitted olives

1 cup plum tomatoes

fresh basil leaves

Method

Mix oil and garlic. Spread on surface of bread. Bake at 400° for 8-10 minutes or until brown. Cool. Mix cream cheese and Parmesan cheese with electric mixer on medium speed until blended. Stir in olives. Spread on cooled bread halves. Top with tomato and basil leaves. Cut into slices.

Makes two dozen

Ingredients

1 packet yeast

1½ cups lukewarm water

1 tablespoon sugar

2 teaspoons salt

4 cups flour

1 egg yolk

Coarse salt

Method

Dissolve yeast in 1½ cups lukewarm water. Add sugar and salt; stir until dissolved. Add flour; mix well. Turn dough onto floured board. Knead for about 5 minutes. Roll into thin strips; shape into pretzels. Place on well greased cookie sheet. Beat egg yolk with 1 tablespoon water; brush on pretzels. Sprinkle generously with coarse salt. Bake in 425F degree oven for 15 to 20 minutes.

St. Lucia Buns

(Parents encourage kids to help)

Ingredients

2 packets active dry yeast

½ cup warm water

2/3 cup lukewarm milk (scalded then cooled)

½ cup sugar

½ cup butter, softened

2 eggs

½ teaspoon ground cardamom

1 teaspoon salt

½ teaspoon powdered saffron

5-1/2 cups all-purpose flour

½ cup raisins

1 egg slightly beaten

1 tablespoon water

2 tablespoons sugar

Method

1. Dissolve yeast in warm water. Stir in milk, sugar, butter, 2 eggs, cardamom, salt, saffron, and 3 cups of flour. Beat until smooth. Stir in enough of the remaining flour to make dough easy to handle.

2. Turn dough onto lightly floured surface; knead until smooth. Place in greased bowl, cover, and let rise until double.

3. Punch down dough; divide into 24 parts. Shape each piece into an S-shaped rope; curve both ends into a coil. Place a raisin in the center of each coil. Place rolls on greased cookie sheet. Brush tops lightly with butter; let rise until doubled.

4. Mix 1 egg and 1 tablespoon water; brush buns lightly. Sprinkle with 2 tablespoons sugar. Bake at 350 degrees for 15-20 minutes. Makes 24 buns.

If you prefer to use a **bread machine** use: 1 teaspoon active dry yeast, 2 cups bread flour, ½ teaspoon dried lemon peel, 1 teaspoon salt, 1 ½ teaspoon sugar, 1 egg, 1 ½ tablespoon butter, ½ cup warm milk, 1 ½ cup ounce warm water, 3 tablespoon chopped almonds, 2 ½ tablespoons raisins.

Load all the ingredients into the bread machine after mixing them together. Start it up according to machine and at the end of the cycle add the almonds and raisins. For the twist in the recipe, add 1 and half teaspoon of cinnamon to the mix. Enjoy it for it is delicious.

Whole Wheat Banana Bread

· ·

Ingredients

1½ cups all-purpose flour

½ cup whole wheat flour

¾ teaspoon baking soda

½ teaspoon salt

1 cup sugar

¼ cup butter, softened

2 large eggs

3 ripe bananas, mashed

1/3 cup 2% plain Greek yogurt

1 teaspoon vanilla extract

½ teaspoon cinnamon

Cooking spray

Method

1. Combine the flour, baking soda, salt and cinnamon, and stir all together.
2. Place the sugar and butter in a large bowl, and beat with a mixer at medium speed until well blended for about one minute. Add the eggs, one at a time, beating well after each addition. Add banana, yogurt, and vanilla. Beat until blended. Add flour mixture, beat at low speed just until moist. Spoon batter into an 8 ½ x 4½ inch loaf pan coated with cooking spray.
3. Bake at 350 degrees for 1 hour or until a wooden tooth pick inserted in center comes out clean. Cool 10 minutes in pan on a wire rack; remove from pan. Cool completely on wire rack.

Cakes

Almond Cake

Ingredients

1 cup butter or margarine, softened

1 cup granulated sugar

3 eggs

1 can almond filling

2¼ cups all-purpose flour

2 teaspoons baking powder

½ teaspoon salt

Almond glaze:

1 cup confectioners sugar

2 tablespoons light cream

¼ teaspoon almond extract

Method

Preheat over 350°F. Lightly grease and flour 10" tube pan or 12 cup Bundt pan.

Beat butter and granulated sugar with electric mixer until light and fluffy. Add eggs, 1 at a time. Add in almond filling until blended. Stir flour, baking powder and salt. Add to almond mixture alternately with milk beginning and ending with dry ingredients. Beat until blended. Spread batter in prepared pan. Bake 50 to 55 minutes or until cake tester inserted in center comes out clean. Cool in pan in wire rack for 10 minutes. Remove from pan and cool completely on rack.

Glaze

Combine confectioners sugar, cream and almond extract in a small bowl and stir until blended and smooth. Spoon or drizzle over top of cake. Let stand until glaze is set. Yield: 10 to 12 servings.

Caribbean Black Cake

Ingredients

1 16 oz. currants
1 16 oz. jar maraschino cherries, drained
2½ cups dark rum
1 pound dried figs
1 tablespoon Angostura bitters
½ cup boiling water
4 cups flour
2 cups brown sugar
4 tablespoons baking powder
9 large eggs
1 tablespoon nutmeg

1 16 oz. prunes
4 oz. almonds, chopped
1 16 oz. raisins
8 oz. mixed peel
¾ pound brown sugar
2 tablespoons grated lime peel
1 teaspoon ground cloves
2 teaspoons vanilla
1 16 oz. butter, softened
1 teaspoon salt

Method

1. Chop currants, raisins, prunes, figs and cherries. Put in a large bowl with mixed peel and almonds and combine. Sprinkle on bitters and pour rum over mixture. Soak for 24 hours, can be extended to three months.

2. For caramelizing sugar, put brown sugar in heavy pot. Let sugar liquefy. Cook over low heat until dark, stirring constantly, so sugar won't burn. Remove from heat when almost burnt and stir in hot water. Mix well and pour into container for cooking.

3. Preheat oven to 350 degrees F. Stir in lime peel, vanilla, and ¾ pound brown sugar and ½ cup boiling water and set aside. Sift together flour, baking powder and cloves set aside. Mix together butter and sugar until the mixture is light and fluffy. Blend in the eggs one at a time. Stir in dry ingredients when mixed. Stir in fruits.

4. Pour into tins greased and floured. Place pan in large shallow pan of hot water. Bake in preheated oven at 250 degrees for 2 ½ to 3 hours or until a tester inserted and comes out clean. Cool for 24 hours. When cool moisten with rum. Remove from tin and wrap in aluminum foil. Check occasionally and add more rum. Yield 1 large cake.

Carrot Cake and Icing

Ingredients

2 cups sifted flour

2 cups sugar

2 teaspoons baking powder

1½ teaspoons baking soda

2 teaspoons cinnamon

1 teaspoon salt

1½ cup oil

4 eggs

Method

Combine all the above ingredients and beat till smooth.

Add:

1 (8½ oz.) can crushed pineapple, drained

2 cups shredded carrots

1 cup chopped nuts (optional)

Bake in a greased 9 X13 inch pan at 350°F degrees for about 40 minutes or till done. Top with cream cheese icing.

Cream Cheese Icing

1 (8 oz.) package cream cheese

½ cup butter or margarine

2½ cups powdered sugar

1 teaspoon vanilla

Chocolate Cake

Ingredients

8 oz. butter

2 1/2 cups white sugar

2 3/4 cup flour

4 eggs

2 teaspoons baking soda

1/2 teaspoon baking powder

1 cup cocoa powder

1/2 teaspoon salt

Method

1. Melt 1 cup cocoa powder in 2 cups boiling water. Let cool.
2. Cream butter and sugar adding sugar gradually. Add eggs one at a time beating after each.
3. Mix flour, baking soda, baking powder, and salt together.
4. Add mixture to egg batter with chocolate mix. (Alternate portions of some flour and some chocolate until finish).

Bake in an 8 X 9 inch round cake pan for 350 degrees for 35 minutes until golden brown. Insert a knife to test cake before removing from oven.

Cinnamon Apple Coffee Cake

. . . .

Ingredients

2 cups flour

1 teaspoon baking powder

1 teaspoon baking soda

1 teaspoon cinnamon

1/2 teaspoon salt

2/3 cup butter (that would be a stick and some)

1 cup sugar

1/2 cup brown sugar

1 egg

1 cup buttermilk or sour milk*

1 cup peeled, cored, and chopped green apples

Topping:

1/2 cup brown sugar

½ to 3/4 cup nuts, chopped

1 teaspoon cinnamon

1/2 teaspoon nutmeg

Method

Preheat oven to 350 degrees. Butter a 9 x 13 baking dish. Combine the first 5 ingredients.

Cream the butter, sugars, and egg. Mix in the dry mixture alternately with the buttermilk into the creamed mixture. Fold in the chopped apple. Put into the baking dish. Mix the topping ingredients and sprinkle over the batter. Bake for 35-40 minutes.

You make sour milk in 5 minutes by combining 1 tablespoon of vinegar with 1 cup of milk and letting it stand for 5 minutes.

Dark Fruitcake

Ingredients

½ cup softened butter

1-1/3 cups brown sugar

2 ¾ cups flour

5 eggs

½ cup strong coffee

Juice and grated rind of 1 lemon

Juice and grated rind of 1 orange

½ cup tart jelly, such as currant

½ cup molasses

1½ pound raisins; 1 pound currants;

½ pound citron; ½ pound dates;

1 teaspoon nutmeg; ½ teaspoon mace;

1 teaspoon cinnamon, ½ teaspoon baking soda

1 ½ teaspoon baking powder

1/3 cup blanched, slivered almonds to sprinkle on top

Method

Cream butter and sugar; add molasses, coffee, lemon rind, orange rind, and jelly.

Add well beaten eggs. Reserve 1 cup flour and mix with fruits. Mix and sift remaining dry ingredients and add to creamed mixture. Stir in remaining fruits. Bake in greased paper lined pans. Sprinkle almonds on top. Bake at 300 degrees for 2 hours with a shallow pan of water on a lower rack of the oven for steaming. Remove water and bake 1 more hour or until cake tests for doneness. Makes 5 pounds of cake or 3 4X8 loaves.

Eggless Coconut Cake

Ingredients

1 pound flour

1/2 pound butter

1 pound white sugar

2 tablespoons baking powder

1 tablespoon vanilla extract

1 tablespoon almond extract

dash of cinnamon and nutmeg

½ cup water

1 coconut grated (or buy 14 oz. package in supermarket)

Method

Cream sugar and butter together. Mix flour and the remaining ingredients together and add to the sugar batter. Grease pan and bake at 325 degrees or till brown. Test cake to see when it's done.

German Sweet Chocolate Cake

. . . .

Ingredients

1 (4 oz.) package sweet cooking chocolate

1/2 cup boiling water

1 cup butter

2 cups sugar

4 egg yolks, beaten

1 teaspoon vanilla

2 1/2 cups cake flour

1 teaspoon baking soda

1/2 teaspoon salt

1 cup buttermilk

4 egg whites, stiffly beaten

Method

1. Melt chocolate in boiling water, and then cool.
2. Cream butter and sugar until fluffy.
3. Add egg yolks, beating each one at a time. Blend in vanilla and chocolate.
4. Sift flour with baking soda and salt.
5. Add dry mixture alternately with buttermilk, mixing well after each addition. Fold in beaten egg whites.
6. Pour into three 8X8 inch prepared cake pans. Bake at 350° for 35-40 minutes.

FROSTING:

3 egg yolks

1 cup evaporated milk

1 cup sugar

1 tablespoon butter

1 1/2 cup flaked coconut

1 cup chopped pecans

1 teaspoon vanilla

Beat eggs, milk, sugar, and butter. Cook over medium heat for about 10 minutes, stirring until mixture thickens. Remove from heat; add coconut, pecans, and vanilla. Beat until cool and of spreading consistency. Frost cake between layers, top, and sides.

Gingerbread Cake With Peach Whipped Cream

. . . .

Ingredients

1½ cup oat flour

¾ cup whole grain pastry flour

2 teaspoons baking powder

1 teaspoon ground ginger

1 teaspoon ground cinnamon

½ teaspoon ground cloves

1 pinch salt

1/3 cup canola oil

¼ cup light molasses

1 ¼ cups hot tap water

1 teaspoon baking soda

1 large egg

1 large egg yolk

¼ cup sugar

½ cup heavy cream, chilled

3 tablespoons peach all-fruit preserves, melted

Method

1. Preheat the oven to 350°F. Coat an 8X8 inch round cake pan with cooking spray.
2. In a medium bowl, mix the oat flour, pastry flour, baking powder, ginger, cinnamon, cloves, and salt.
3. In a large bowl, mix the oil and molasses.
4. In a 2 cup glass measuring cup, mix the water and baking soda. Whisk into the molasses mixture.

5. Gradually whisk in the flour mixture. Whisk in the egg, egg yolk, and sugar. Pour into the prepared pan.

6. Bake for 30 minutes, or until a wooden pick inserted in the center comes out clean. Cool on a rack for 10 minutes. Remove from the pan and place on the rack to cool completely.

7. Place the cream and preserves in a medium bowl. Using an electric mixer on medium speed beat until soft peaks form. Serve over wedges of the cake.

8. This gingerbread cake (minus the cream topping) keeps well in a zip-top bag at room temperature for 1 day or in the freezer for 1 month. The whipped cream will keep in a covered container in the refrigerator for 1 day.

TIP: Replace the peach preserves with apricot, raspberry, or cherry for a flavor variation.

Light Carrot Cake

Ingredients

¾ cup sugar

½ cup vegetable oil

1/3 cup orange juice concentrate

4 eggs beaten

2½ cup all-purpose flour

1 teaspoon baking powder

1 teaspoon ground cinnamon

1 teaspoon nutmeg

½ teaspoon vanilla

½ teaspoon ground allspice

¼ teaspoon baking soda

1/8 teaspoon salt

3 cups grated carrots

Confectioners sugar for dusting

Method

1. Blend sugar and oil together in a large bowl; add eggs, salt, and mix well. Stir in carrots and orange juice, and add in dry ingredients.

2. Pour into a greased 9X13 pan, and then spread the mixture in the baking pan. Bake 375 degrees for 50 minutes or until a toothpick inserted near the center comes out clean. Cool; dust with confectioner's sugar. Yield: 12 servings.

Pistachio Bundt Cake

Ingredients

1 package (18-1/4 oz.) yellow cake mix
1 package (3.4 oz. each) instant pistachio pudding mix
1 cup water
4 eggs
¾ cup vegetable oil

GLAZE:
1 cup confectioners' sugar
1 tablespoon butter, softened
2 to 3 tablespoons milk

NOTE: This is a moist cake, pretty mint green. The outside browns nicely to form a slightly crunchy crust. The cake slices beautifully and would make a fun dessert.

Method

In a large bowl, combine the cake mix, pudding mix, water, eggs and oil; beat on low speed for 30 seconds. Beat on medium for 2 minutes. Pour into a greased and floured 10-inch fluted tube pan. Bake at 350°F for 60-70 minutes or until a toothpick inserted near the center comes out clean. Cool for 10 minutes before removing from pan to a wire rack to cool completely.

In small bowl, combine the glaze ingredients, adding enough milk to reach desired consistency. Drizzle over cake. Yield: 12 servings.

NOTE:
Adding 1 cup of sour cream 2 teaspoon almond extract to the batter makes the cake very moist. You can replace yellow cake mix with 3 boxes of jiffy yellow cake mix.

If you like a nut swirl pistachio cake, use half of the mix in Bundt pan and add chopped walnuts and cinnamon in the middle and add the second half and bake.

Pumpkin Bundt Cake

· ·

Ingredients

2 cups all-purpose unbleached flour

1 cup white whole wheat flour

1½ teaspoons baking powder

1 teaspoon baking soda

½ teaspoon salt

1½ teaspoons cinnamon

½ teaspoon nutmeg

¼ teaspoon ginger

1 cup soymilk

1¼ cup pumpkin puree

½ cup canola or vegetable oil

1 teaspoon pure vanilla extract

½ cup light brown sugar, packed

½ cup honey

2 eggs

¾ cup walnuts, chopped

1 apple, chopped

Method

Mix the dry ingredients together. Beat eggs with sugar. Add the wet ingredients to the eggs and sugar mixture slowly, and then stir contents together. Fold in apples or place on the bottom of the Bundt pan for a prettier look. Fold in walnuts.

Pour into oiled or sprayed Bundt pan with a dusting of flour. Bake 400° F for first 10 min., and then reduce heat to 350° F and bake for 45 minutes more. Test with toothpick when done. Cool in Bundt pan for 10 minutes before removing onto a cooling rack. Garnish with chopped apple.

Pumpkin Cheesecake

- -

Ingredients

Crust

2 cups whole wheat bread crumbs

¼ cup sugar

¼ cup light brown sugar

8 tablespoons (1 stick) unsalted butter, melted

½ teaspoon salt

Filling

1 ½ pounds cream cheese, softened

2 cups cooked, mashed pumpkin

1 cup sugar

1 tablespoon vanilla extract

1 teaspoon ground cinnamon

1 teaspoon ground nutmeg

1 teaspoon ground ginger

Zest of 1 lemon

4 large eggs

1 cup heavy cream

Method

Preheat oven to 500°F. To make the crust, combine the whole wheat bread crumbs, sugars, butter, and salt in a medium bowl until the bread crumbs are thoroughly coated. Press the mixture into the bottom of a 9-inch spring form pan.

TIP: This cake freezes well for up to 3 months

Cream the cheese, pumpkin, sugar, vanilla extract, spices, and lemon zest together. Beat in the eggs, one at a time, then the cream, and blend until smooth (if the batter is still lumpy, you can press it through a sieve). Pour the batter into the prepared pan, place in the oven, and immediately reduce the heat to 325°F.

Bake for 45 minutes to 1 hour, or until the filling is set. Cool thoroughly at room temperature before chilling.

Red Velvet Cake

. . . .

Ingredients

Vegetable oil for the pans

2 1/2 cups flour

1½ cup sugar

1 teaspoon baking soda

1 teaspoon salt

1 teaspoon cocoa powder

1 1/2 cup vegetable oil

1 cup buttermilk, at room temperature

2 large eggs, room temperature

2 teaspoons red food coloring (1 ounce)

1 teaspoon white distilled vinegar

1 teaspoon vanilla extract

Vanilla Cream Cheese Frosting, recipe follows

Crushed pecans, for garnish

Method

Preheat oven to 350 degrees F. Lightly oil and flour three 9x1½ inch cake pans.

Sift together in a bowl, flour, sugar, baking powder, salt, and cocoa powder. In another large bowl, whisk together oil, buttermilk, eggs, food coloring, vinegar, and vanilla.

Using a standing mixer, mix the dry ingredients into the wet ingredients until just combined and a smooth batter is formed.

Divide the cake batter evenly among the prepared cake pans. Place the pans in the oven evenly spaced apart. Bake, turning the pans halfway through the cooking, until the cake pulls away from the side of the pans, and a toothpick inserted in the center of the cakes comes out clean, about 30 minutes.

Remove the cakes from the oven and run a knife around the edges to loosen them from the sides of the pans. One at a time, invert the cakes onto a plate and then re-invert the cakes onto a cooling rack, rounded-sides up. Let cool completely.

Frost the cake. Place one layer, rounded-side down, in the middle of a rotating cake stand. Using a palette knife or a spatula spread some of the cream cheese frosting over the top of the cake. Spread enough frosting to make a ¼ to ½ inch layer. Carefully set another layer on top, rounded-side down, and repeat. Top with remaining layer and cover the entire cake with the remaining frosting. Sprinkle the top with the pecans.

Vanilla Cream Cheese Frosting:
1 8-ounce package cream cheese, softened,
4 cups confectioners' sugar
1 cup unsalted butter, softened,
1-teaspoon pure vanilla extract

In a standing mixer with paddle attachment, or with an electric mixer in a large bowl, mix the cream cheese, sugar, and butter on low speed until incorporated. Increase the speed to high, and mix until light and fluffy, about five minutes. Occasionally turn the mixer off and scrape the sides of the bowl with a rubber spatula.

Reduce the speed of the mixer to low. Add the vanilla, increase the speed to high and mix until fluffy and scrape the bowl occasionally. Store in refrigerator until somewhat stiff before using.

Sugar Cakes

. . . .

Ingredients

4 cups of grated coconut

1 cup water

½ teaspoon cream of tartar

3 cups granulated sugar

1 teaspoon almond extract

1-1/2 teaspoons ginger

Food coloring

Method

In a saucepan boil sugar and water to form a light syrup. When the bubbles are the size of small pearls, gradually add coconut, cream of tartar and ginger.

Frequently stir mixture, when the coconut mixture comes away clean from the sides of the pan quite easily, remove from heat and stir with a wooden spoon for 3 to 5 minutes.

Add almond extract and food coloring if desired. Drop by spoon on a greased cookie sheet. Allow to completely harden. Makes 30.

Cookies

Apple Cranberry Breakfast Cookies

. . . .

*This is an excellent breakfast option or a tasty snack for those
on the run! And they're low in fat and high in fiber.*

Ingredients

¼ cup no-salt soft margarine

¾ cup dark brown sugar, packed

2 large eggs

½ cup unsweetened applesauce

1 ½ cup whole wheat flour

½ teaspoon table salt

½ teaspoon ground cinnamon

1 teaspoon baking soda

1 ½ cup uncooked quick oats

½ cup dried apples, chopped

½ cup dried cranberries

½ cup chopped walnuts

butter flavored cooking spray

Method

Preheat oven to 350°

1. Combine margarine and sugar in a bowl. Beat with an electric mixer until light and fluffy, about 1 minute. Add eggs and beat for 30 seconds. Add applesauce and beat just to mix.
2. In another bowl, stir together flour, salt, cinnamon, and baking soda. Add to mixer and beat to form batter. Add oats, apples, cranberries, and walnuts; combine by hand.

3. Line cookie sheet with parchment paper or coat with cooking spray. Drop batter by heaping tablespoons 1 inch apart. Bake until cookies are lightly browned and firm, about 13-15 minutes.

4. Remove from oven and let stand 10 minutes. Move to wire rack and cool completely. Yields about 30 cookies. These cookies store well in an airtight container or plastic bag in the freezer.

Big Chocolate Chip Cookies

. . . .

Ingredients

1 cup butter softened

1 cup packed brown sugar

¾ cup sugar

2 eggs

1 ½ teaspoon vanilla extract

2 2/3 cups all purpose flour

1 1/4 teaspoon baking soda

1 teaspoon salt

1 package 12 ounce semisweet chocolate chips

2 cups coarsely chopped walnuts, toasted

Method

1. In a large bowl, cream the butter, brown sugar and sugar until light and fluffy. Beat in eggs and vanilla. Combine the flour, baking soda and salt; gradually add to creamed mixture and mix well. Stir in chocolate chips and walnuts.

2. Place the dough in refrigerator over night in an airtight container or use the same large bowl.

3. Shape quarter cupfuls of dough into balls.

4. To bake, place dough balls 3 inches apart on parchment paper-lined baking sheets. Press a shallow indentation in the center of each with your thumb, reshaping sides to smooth any cracks. Let stand at room temperature for 30 minutes or less.

5. Bake the first batch at 400o degrees for 10-12 minutes or until edges are golden brown. Reduce the heat to 365o degrees to bake the balance of the cookie dough. Cool for 2 minutes before removing from pans to wire racks; cool.

Chocolate Dipped Heart Cookies

. . . .

Ingredients

1 roll (16.5 oz.) refrigerated sugar cookies

¼ to ½ cup all-purpose flour

1 ½ cups semisweet chocolate chips

1 tablespoon shortening

Colored sugar

Method

1. Heat oven 350°F. Remove half of cookie dough from wrapper; refrigerate remaining dough until needed. Sprinkle about 3 tablespoons of the flour onto work surface; coat sides of half of dough with flour. With rolling pin, roll out dough to ¼ inch thickness, adding additional flour as needed to prevent sticking.

2. With floured 3 inch heart shaped cookie cutter, cut out hearts. Gently brush excess flour from hearts; place 2 inches apart on ungreased cookie sheets. Repeat with remaining half of dough.

3. Bake 7 to 9 minutes or until light golden brown. Cool 1 minute; remove from cookie sheets to cooling racks. Cool completely, about 15 minutes.

4. In 1 quart saucepan, heat chocolate chips and shortening over low heat, stirring occasionally, until melted and smooth. Remove from heat. Dip half of each cookie into melted chocolate, allowing excess chocolate to drip off; place on waxed paper lined cookie sheets. Sprinkle with colored sugar.

Christmas Oreo Truffles

. . . .

*These truffles are easy and delicious. You can't go wrong with Oreo,
cream cheese, and chocolate. I made these last Christmas and they were
a huge hit simple to make and everyone asked for the recipe.*

Ingredients

1 (16 oz.) package Oreo chocolate sandwich cookies, divided

1 (8 oz.) package cream cheese, softened

2 (8 oz.) packages semisweet baking chocolate, melted

1 teaspoon vanilla

1 teaspoon almond extract

Method

1. Crush 9 of the cookies to fine crumbs in the food processor and reserve for later use. (Cookies can also be finely crushed in a reusable plastic bag using a rolling pin). Crush the remaining 27 cookies to fine crumbs and place in medium bowl. Add softened cream cheese, vanilla and almond extract and mix until well blended. Roll cookie mixture into 42 balls, about 1 inch in diameter.
2. Dip balls in melted chocolate; place on wax paper covered baking sheet. (Any leftover chocolate can be stored at room temperature for another use).
3. If you wish, you may use ½ teaspoon of melted chocolate on each truffle after you roll in the crumbs. Sprinkle with reserved cookie crumbs.
4. Refrigerate until firm, about one hour. Store leftover truffles, covered in refrigerator.

Cowboy Cookies

. . . .

Ingredients

1 cup shortening

1 cup sugar

1 cup brown sugar

2 eggs

2 cups flour

2 cups quick oats

1 teaspoon baking powder

1 (12 oz.) chocolate chips

Method

Cream together shortening, sugars, and eggs. Add remaining ingredients. Mix well. Drop by teaspoonfuls unto ungreased cookie sheet. Bake at 350°F for 10-12 minutes.

Healthy Cereal Cookies

Ingredients

- 1 cup margarine at room temperature
- 1 cup white sugar
- 1 cup brown sugar
- 1 cup vegetable oil
- 2 eggs
- 1 teaspoon vanilla
- 3 cups flour
- 1 1/2 cups quick oats
- 1 teaspoon baking soda
- 1 teaspoon salt
- 1 teaspoon cream of tartar
- 1 cup Rice Krispies
- 1 cup coconut
- 1 cup chocolate chips

Method

In a mixing bowl, cream together, butter, sugars, and oil. Add eggs and vanilla. In a separate bowl, combine flour, baking soda, salt and cream of tartar. Add to egg mixture. Stir in Rice Krispies, oatmeal, coconut, and chocolate chips.

Drop by teaspoonfuls onto ungreased cookie sheet. Bake on lower shelf of oven at 350° for 5 minutes. Move cookie sheet to middle of oven. Continue baking for 10 minutes or until lightly browned. Remove from sheet to cool.

> **TIP:** More than one cookie sheet can be used to speed the process. While one or two cookie sheets can be used side by side in the oven, prepare another cookie sheet.

Lemon Pecan Meringue

. . . .

Ingredients

½ cup pecans

3 egg whites, at room temperature

Pinch of cream of tartar

½ cup sugar

1 tablespoon grated lemon zest

½ teaspoon vanilla extract

Directions

1. Preheat oven to 350°F. Put pecans on a baking sheet and toast in oven, shaking pan once or twice, until nuts smell fragrant, about 5 minutes. Cool and finely chop.
2. Reduce oven temperature to 200°F. Line 2 baking sheets with parchment paper or foil.
3. Put egg whites and cream of tartar in the clean bowl of an electric mixer. Beat on medium speed until whites form soft peaks when beaters are lifted, 3 to 4 minutes. Gradually add sugar, beating until whites hold stiff peaks when beaters are lifted, 3 to 4 minutes more. Fold in toasted nuts, lemon zest, and vanilla.
4. Spoon meringue into a large ziplock bag, cut off a small piece of a corner, and squeeze meringue into 1 1/2-inch rounds on baking sheets.
5. Bake without opening the oven door for 1 hour and 15 minutes. Turn off oven and let meringues sit in the oven until cool, at least 1 hour or as long as overnight (you can turn off the oven just before going to bed and let the cookies cool in there until morning).

6. Serve immediately or store in an airtight container for about a day. The cookies will keep longest if the humidity is low. Makes about 60 cookies.

TIP: Avoid making meringue cookies on a humid or wet day because the moisture in the air will be absorbed by the meringue and make the cookies sticky.

Melting Moments

. . . .

Ingredients

Batter

1 cup butter

¼ cup powdered sugar

1 cup flour

¾ cup cornstarch

1 teaspoon vanilla extract

1 dash salt

Frosting

1 (3 oz.) cream cheese

1 cup powdered sugar

½ teaspoon almond extract

Method

Cream the butter, sugar until creamy with a hand mixer. Beat in vanilla extract. Add flour and cornstarch, and salt to make batter in a bowl. Shape into one inch round balls. Bake on greased cookie sheet, one inch apart at 375 degrees F for 10-15 minutes.

Remove from oven. Let stand a few minutes to cool. In the meantime, prepare frosting and decorate. Let frosting on cookies harden.

Rum Balls

Ingredients

1 cup fine vanilla wafer crumbs

1 cup finely chopped pecans

1 cup confectioners' sugar

2 tablespoons unsweetened cocoa powder

¼ cup bourbon

1 tablespoon plus 1 ½ teaspoons light corn syrup

confectioners' sugar for sifting

Method

1. Thoroughly combine 1 cup crushed vanilla wafer crumbs, chopped pecans, 1 cup confectioners' sugar, and the cocoa.

2. In a separate bowl, blend the bourbon and corn syrup. Stir this bourbon mixture into the dry mixture; blend well.

3. Cover and chill for at least a few hours. Sift about ½ to 1 cup of confectioners' sugar on a cookie sheet. Shape small bits of the dough into balls and roll them in the confectioners' sugar.

4. Store in refrigerator in tightly covered containers. Make these a few days in advance for best flavor, and roll in confectioners' sugar again before serving, if desired. These can be frozen for longer storage. Makes about 3 dozen bourbon balls.

Tea-Time Lemon Sandwich Cookies

. . . .

Ingredients

1 cup butter, softened

¾ cup vanilla ice cream, softened

1 ½ teaspoons grated lemon peel

2 cups all purpose or unbleached flour

¼ cup sugar

Filling:

¾ cup powdered sugar

¼ cup butter, softened

1 teaspoon grated lemon peel

1 to 3 teaspoons fresh lemon juice

1 to 2 drops yellow food color, if desired

Method

1. Combine 1 cup butter, ice cream and 1 1/2 teaspoons lemon peel in a large bowl; blend well. Lightly spoon flour into measuring cup; level off. Add flour; mix well. Cover with plastic wrap; refrigerate 1 hour for easier handling.

2. Heat oven to 375°F. On lightly floured surface, roll dough to 1/8 inch thick. Cut with floured ½ inch round cookie cutter. Coat both sides of cutout cookies with sugar; place 1 inch apart on ungreased cookie sheets. With fork, prick each cookie 2 to 4 times.

3. Bake at 375°F for 7 to 8 minutes or until slightly puffed but not brown. Cool 1 minute; remove from cookie sheets. Cool 10 minutes or until completely cooled.

4. Prepare filling in a small bowl, combine powdered sugar, 1/4 cup butter, 1 teaspoon lemon peel and enough lemon juice for desired spreading consistency; beat at medium speed until smooth. Add food color; mix until well blended. Spread approximately 1/2 teaspoon filling between 2 cooled cookies. Makes two dozen cookies. 1 Serving (1 Cookie) Calories 80

Desserts

Apple Ring Pull Apart

· ·

Ingredients

½ cup apple jelly

¼ cup chopped walnuts or pecans

½ cup firmly packed brown sugar

½ teaspoon cinnamon

1 large apple, peeled

2 (12-oz.) cans refrigerated biscuits

¼ cup margarine or butter, melted

Method

1. Heat oven to 350°F. Grease 12 cup fluted tube cake pan. Spoon apple jelly evenly over bottom of greased pan; sprinkle with walnuts. In small bowl, combine brown sugar and cinnamon; set aside. Cut apple into quarters; remove core. Slice each quarter into 5 slices.

2. Separate dough into 20 biscuits; flatten each slightly. Wrap 1 biscuit around each apple slice; pinch edges to seal and completely cover apple slice. Dip each in margarine; roll in brown sugar cinnamon mixture. Stand biscuits on end in greased pan. Drizzle with any remaining margarine; sprinkle with any remaining brown sugar cinnamon mixture.

3. Bake at 350°F. for 30 to 40 minutes or until golden brown. Cool upright in pan for 8 minutes; invert onto serving plate. Spoon any additional topping over baked ring. Serve warm.

Brazilian Coconut Flan

. . . .

Ingredients

1 2/3 cups unsweetened shredded coconut

1 cup full fat whole milk

3 tablespoons unsalted (sweet) butter softened

2 cups caster (superfine) sugar plus extra for dusting

18 egg yolks

Method

Heat oven at 425° degrees

1. Combine coconut and milk in a bowl. Let it stand for 15 minutes.
2. Grease a 9 inch ring mould with some of the butter and lightly dust with caster sugar.
3. Put the remaining butter in a large bowl. Add the sugar and soaked coconut and mix until thoroughly combined.
4. With a wooden spoon gently stir in egg yolks, one at a time. When the ingredients are combined, cover the bowl with a clean dishtowel and leave the mixture to stand in a cool place for one hour.
5. Tip the coconut mixture into the prepared ring mould and place in the center of a deep roasting pan. Pour in enough warm water to come halfway outside of the mould. Place the mould in a cold oven.
6. Bake flan for 1 hour or until surface is dark and golden. Remove from oven and leave to cool in the water in the roasting pan.
7. When flan is cold, loosen the edges with a knife. Cover with a serving platter and turn mould gently upside down. Lift off the ring mould and do not touch the top of the flan. Serve and cut in thick slices.

Bread Pudding With Brandy Sauce

. . . .

Ingredients

1 pound day old white sandwich bread crusts removed

4 cups milk

1 cup coconut crème

5 eggs, slightly beaten

½ teaspoon salt

¼ cup sugar

½ teaspoon ground cinnamon

¼ cup crushed almonds

½ cup raisins

¼ butter, melted

Method

Break the bread into small pieces, place in a bowl and pour the milk over. Soak for 10 minutes. Mash bread, and add all the other ingredients mixing well. Pour the pudding into a well greased 2½ quart casserole and set in a larger pan. Pour about 1 inch water into the larger pan. Bake in preheated 350°F oven for 1½ hours. Cool, pour brandy sauce over the entire pudding and serve.

Brandy Sauce:

¼ cup butter, at room temperature

½ cup sugar

2 tablespoons brandy

¼ cup milk

2 eggs, separated

Cream together the butter and sugar. Add the brandy, milk, and egg yolks. Mix well. Pour into a double boiler and cook over hot water until slightly thick, stirring with a wooden spoon to prevent lumps. Cool.

Beat the egg whites until frothy, then fold into the brandy mixture. Stir and pour sauce over the pudding. Serves 6 to 8

Fruit Cup With Citrus Sauce

. . . .

Ingredients

¾ cup orange juice

¼ cup white wine or white grape juice

2 tablespoons lemon juice

1 tablespoon sugar

1 ½ cups fresh or frozen canteloupe balls

1 cup halved green grapes

1 cup halved fresh strawberries

Fresh mint, optional

Method

In a small bowl, combine the orange juice, wine or grape juice, lemon juice and sugar; mix well. In a large bowl, combine the fruit; add juice mixture and toss to coat. Cover and refrigerate for 2-3 hours, stirring occasionally. Garnish with mint if desired. Yield 6 servings.

Fruit Salad

· ·

Ingredients

1 (12 oz.) pack cranberries

3 medium apples

1 cup green seedless grapes, halved

1 pint whipping cream

1 cup miniature marshmallows

1 cup sugar

½ cup chopped pecans

NOTE: Berries can be pulsed in a food processor instead of a blender.

Method

Chop berries in blender. Dice unpeeled apples. Combine berries, apples, and sugar. Refrigerate, covered, for 2 to 3 hours. Spoon off excess liquid. Whip cream; fold in cranapple mixture, marshmallows, grapes and pecans.

Packaged "Cool Whip" can be used instead of whipping your own cream, but reduce sugar to ½ cup.

Ice Cream Cupcakes

• •

Ingredients

Paper cupcake liners

Muffin tin

12 chocolate sandwich cookies

Mint chocolate chip ice cream

1 cup whipping cream

1 tablespoon cocoa powder

1 tablespoon powdered sugar

Method

Place 12 paper cupcake liners in muffin tin.

Crumble one cookie in each cupcake liner.

Place scoop of ice cream in each liner. Freeze until solid.

Meanwhile, whip cream until slightly thickened, add cocoa and powdered sugar; continue whipping until soft peaks form.

Frost each cupcake with cocoa whipped cream. Freeze until ready to serve. Place extra cupcakes in airtight container; store in freezer up to one week.

Pineapple Pretzel Salad

. . . .

Ingredients

2 cups crushed pretzels

1/2 cup sugar

1 stick butter

1 (8 oz.) package cream cheese

1/2 cup sugar

1 (20 oz.) can pineapple with juice

1 (8 oz.) carton whipped topping

Method

Melt butter in 9x13 pan. Mix in sugar and pretzels. Bake at 400 degrees for 8 minutes. Stir; turn off oven and leave in until cool. Mix together the cream cheese, sugar and pineapple with juice. Fold in whipped topping. Before serving add pretzel mixture.

Pineapple Sherbet

Ingredients

1 egg beaten

1 cup sugar

1 teaspoon lemon extract

1 teaspoon vanilla extract

1 cup crushed pineapple

2 cups milk (part cream if preferred richer)

Method

Mix all ingredients together and freeze in an 8X8 inch pan. Stir well every hour. Do this three times.

Tiramisu Smoothie

Ingredients

1 cup (8 oz.) Wisconsin Mascarpone Cheese

(Italian cream cheese)

1 cup vanilla ice cream

2 tablespoons milk

3 cups chocolate ice cream

1 cup brewed espresso or strong coffee, chilled

4 teaspoons unsweetened cocoa powder

4 teaspoons confectioners' sugar

4 biscotti (vanilla)

Method

Place Mascarpone, vanilla ice cream and milk in a blender container. Blend until smooth and creamy. Pour mixture into bowl or pitcher, set aside.

Place chocolate ice cream and espresso in blender container. Blend until smooth.

Divide chocolate mixture evenly among 4 glasses. Top chocolate mixture with Mascarpone mixture.

In a small bowl, combine cocoa powder and confectioners' sugar. Sift mixture evenly over each glass and garnish with a biscotti. Serve immediately.

Dis and Dat

Avocado-Cheese Dip

Ingredients

1 avocado, peeled and cut into pieces

1 (3 oz.) package cream cheese

1 tablespoon lemon juice

salt to taste

1 to 2 cloves garlic, peeled and cut into pieces

Method

Blend all ingredients until smooth. Chill in refrigerator and serve with crackers.

Bajan Fish Spice

Ingredients

Here is a typical spice blend from Barbados, where it is rubbed into fillets of flying fish before grilling, broiling, or steaming. Whole red snapper or other rockfish can be substituted.

½ yellow onion, chopped enough for 3 to 4 pounds fish

1 garlic clove, minced

2 teaspoons paprika

½ teaspoon cayenne or other ground red chili pepper

½ teaspoon ground thyme or dried thyme leaves

2-3 teaspoons fresh limejuice

2 teaspoons vegetable oil

salt and ground pepper

Method

Combine all the ingredients in a blender or food processor, including salt and pepper to taste. Puree until smooth. To use, cut a diagonal slits along the sides of a whole cleaned fish and rub the seasoning mixture into the slits, or rub the mixture on fish fillets. Cover and refrigerate at least 30 minutes or up to several hours.

Barbecue Sauce

Ingredients

¼ cup vinegar

1 cup brown sugar

1 teaspoon salt

¼ teaspoon pepper

3 teaspoons sugar

½ teaspoon garlic salt

2 teaspoons Worcestershire sauce

1 teaspoon liquid smoke

1 (28 oz.) bottle ketchup

¼ bottle chili sauce

2 to 3 drops of Tabasco sauce

Method

Combine all ingredients store in refrigerator for up to 4 weeks.

Basic Red Barbecue Sauce

· ·

Ingredients

1 cup ketchup

¼ cup cider or red wine vinegar

3 tablespoons firmly packed brown sugar

2 garlic cloves, minced

1 tablespoon dry or prepared mustard

1 teaspoon Worcestershire sauce

½ teaspoon cayenne pepper or Tabasco sauce or other hot pepper sauce

½ yellow onion, finely chopped (optional)

Makes about 1¾ cups; enough for 3 pounds meat

Method

Combine all the ingredients in a small saucepan. Bring to a boil, reduce the heat to low, and cook until thickened and flavors are blended, about 5 minutes. Adjust the vinegar, sugar, and hot pepper to suit your taste. For best results make up to a week in advance. Store, covered tightly, in the refrigerator for up to a month.

Chow Chow

. . . .

Ingredients

20 green tomatoes or unripe winter tomatoes
4 white onions
6-8 green and/or red bell peppers, seeded
6 cucumbers, or 1 large bottle sour gherkins (Mexican product)
2 gallons chopped fresh vegetables
small fresh chiles, to taste
½ cup salt

For syrup:
8 cups distilled white vinegar
2 tablespoons ground turmeric
2 tablespoons mustard seeds
1 ½ cup sugar
1 tablespoon celery seeds

Method

Coarsely chop tomatoes, white onions, bell pepper and cucumbers. Select vegetables that appeal to you and coarsely chop. Mince the chiles. Place all vegetables in large container and sprinkle with salt. Let stand overnight. Drain in a colander.

In a large pot, stir together all the syrup and bring to a boil, stirring to dissolve the sugar. Add the vegetables and boil, stirring occasionally for 10 minutes. Ladle into sterilized jars and screw on the lids. Let stand in refrigerator at least a week or may stay in a dark area for 6 months.

Ladle the chow chow into hot, sterilized canning jars and fill to within ½ inch to the rim. Wipe rims with clean damp cloth, and seal with lids and rings according to the manufacturer's directions. Check for proper seals, then store in a cool, dark place for up to a year. Store any jars that did not seal properly in the refrigerator for up to 6 months.

Green tomatoes are required in this recipe, but hard tomatoes in most supermarkets in the winter months make fine substitute. Chow chow can be made any time of the year using whatever vegetables available.

Dry Jerk Seasoning

Ingredients

1 teaspoon onion flakes

1 teaspoon onion powder

2 teaspoons ground thyme

2 teaspoons salt

1 teaspoon ground pimento (allspice)

¼ teaspoon ground nutmeg

¼ teaspoon ground cinnamon

2 teaspoons sugar

1 teaspoon cayenne pepper

2 teaspoons dried chives or green onions

Method

Mix together all the ingredients. Store leftovers in a tightly closed glass jar. It will keep its pungency for over a month.

This seasoning mix is excellent to have on hand to sprinkle on cooked or uncooked fish, vegetables, or snacks. It does not have a strong flavor as the rub and the marinade. To increase the heat, add more cayenne.

Guacamole Dip

Ingredients

- 1 package frozen guacamole dip
- 8 oz. cream cheese
- 1 cup sour cream

Method

Mix all ingredients together and spread on bottom of 2 quart bowl. Top with layers of:

Green onions or chives
Shredded lettuce
Diced fresh tomatoes
Shredded cheddar cheese
Serve with taco chips

Ham Swirls

Ingredients

16 thinly sliced boiled ham

Green olives, sliced

1 jar cheese spread (olive or pimento)

Method

Spread the ham slices with the cheese. Put slices of the olives on top of cheese. Start at end of ham and roll as you would a jelly roll. Place toothpicks at ½ inch intervals. Slice between toothpicks and you have an easy appetizer.

Jerk Seasoning

Ingredients

1 teaspoon onion flakes

1 teaspoon ground allspice

1 teaspoon ground ginger

2 teaspoons ground thyme

2 teaspoons salt

1 to 3 teaspoons cayenne pepper

½ teaspoon ground black pepper

1 teaspoon sugar

¼ teaspoon ground cinnamon

3 teaspoon garlic powder or 3 garlic cloves, minced

2 to 3 tablespoons vegetable oil

¼ cup fresh limejuice, rum, coconut milk, or water

Method

Combine all the dry ingredients and mix well. Store in an airtight container. When ready to use, take a couple of tablespoons out for each pound of meat, chicken, or fish and mix. Add the fresh garlic, oil, and liquid just before using. Marinate 1 hour or 2.

Light Creamed Spinach

· ·

Ingredients

9 oz. package frozen chopped spinach

1 teaspoon vegetable oil

2 tablespoons sliced green onions

1/3 cup light sour cream

¼ cup skim milk

2 tablespoons grated Parmesan cheese

2 teaspoons all purpose flour

¼ teaspoon salt

Method

Cook the spinach as directed on the package; drain and press with paper towels to remove all of the moisture.

Meanwhile, heat the oil in a 10 inch nonstick skillet over medium heat. Add the onion and cook for one minute. Whisk the sour cream, milk, Parmesan cheese, flour and salt in a small bowl. Stir into the onions in the skillet. Cook the sauce until bubbly and thick. Stir the spinach into the sauce until well mixed and serve.

Little Meat Balls

. . . .

Ingredients

2 tablespoons butter

1 small onion, minced

1 medium stalk celery, minced

½ pound ground beef

¼ teaspoon curry powder

1 clove garlic, minced

½ cup breadcrumbs

1 egg

½ teaspoon thyme

1 teaspoon pepper

1 tablespoon grated Parmesan cheese

Method

Heat butter in a small skillet. Sauté onion, celery, and garlic until golden brown. Place beef in a bowl; add onion mixture and remaining ingredients. Mix lightly with a fork. For appetizers, shape into 1 inch balls and sauté. Place a toothpick in each before serving.

Red Pepper Sour Cream and Chive Dip

Ingredients

1 cup sour cream

8 oz. cream cheese, softened

1 chopped and diced red pepper

2 tablespoons fresh chives minced

2 tablespoons fresh parsley, minced

1 tablespoon fresh herbs (thyme, basil, oregano)

2 teaspoons fresh garlic, finely minced

1/3 cup blue cheese crumbles

¼ teaspoon red pepper flakes

1/4 teaspoon cracked black pepper

Method

Allow cream cheese to sit at room temperature for 20-30 minutes before using.

In a medium bowl, beat cream cheese using a hand mixer until soft. Add sour cream, blue cheese, and remaining ingredients, mixing well.

Cover and refrigerate one hour before serving.

Serving Suggestion:

Serve accompanied by tortilla chips, celery sticks and cucumber strips, lemon and tomato wedges and a small bowl of hot sauce. Sprinkle vegetables with celery or sea salt and pepper.

Spinach Dip

Ingredients

1 10-oz. package frozen, chopped spinach
1 cup mayonnaise
1 cup sour cream
1 package vegetable soup mix
1 cup water chestnuts, drained and chopped

Method

1. Thaw spinach, and place on paper towel and press until slightly moist.
2. Combine spinach, mayonnaise, sour cream, and vegetable soup mix, then add water chestnuts and mix well.
3. Cover and chill mixture several hours. Serve with assorted raw vegetables. It is also good served as a salad dressing.

Sweet and Crunchy Cream Cheese Spread

Ingredients

1 cup small curd cottage cheese

1-8 oz. package cream cheese, softened

2 tablespoons honey

¼ cup walnuts, chopped

½ cup raisins

Method

In medium bowl, combine all ingredients using a spoon or electric mixer; mix well.

Cover and chill 4 hours or overnight. Serve with toasted bagels, toast or muffins.

Tomato Onion Relish

Ingredients

4 firm tomatoes, chopped
1 yellow onion, finely chopped
1 garlic clove, minced
1 teaspoon salt
¼ teaspoon ground black pepper
Juice of 2 limes or lemons

Method

In a bowl, stir together all of the ingredients and mix well. Let stand one hour to blend the flavors. Store covered in the refrigerator up to 3 days.

This West African condiment is a simple salsa like mixture. It is great with spicy meat sticks. The salsa can be used with meat, chicken or fish.

Vinegar Marinade

. . . .

Ingredients

1 cup distilled white, cider, or red wine vinegar

½ cup water

1 lemon, sliced

1 or 2 tablespoons sugar

1 yellow onion, chopped or sliced

¼ teaspoon Tabasco or other hot pepper sauce

¼ teaspoon ground black pepper

1 tablespoon dried sage, crushed

3 tablespoons tomato paste

Method

Combine all the ingredients in a saucepan. Bring to a boil over medium heat. Reduce the heat to low and simmer 10 to 15 minutes. Let cool and pour over meat in a shallow pan or dish. Cover and refrigerate overnight. Vinegar and lemon juice help tenderize tough cuts of beef, pork, goat, or chicken.

Makes 1 ½ cups; enough for 5-6 pounds meat

Drinks

Avocado Daiquiri
(Dominica)

Ingredients

¼ medium ripe avocado peeled

2 oz. light rum (1/4 cup)

2 oz. gold rum (1/4 cup)

2 oz. simple syrup

½ oz. lime juice

½ oz. lemon juice

½ oz. half and half

1½ cup crushed ice

Method

Puree avocados with all ingredients till smooth. Serve at once over crushed ice.

Bahama Mama

. . . .

Ingredients

½ oz. light rum

2 oz. apple juice

½ oz. cream of coconut

1 oz. orange juice

Dash Triple Sec (orange liqueur)

Dash grenadine

Method

Combine the rum, apple juice, cream of coconut, orange juice, Triple Sec, and grenadine in a blender. Process for about 30 seconds, then strain over crushed ice in Collins glass.

Serves 1

Banana Daiquiri

Ingredients

- 1½ oz. light rum
- 1 tablespoon Triple Sec (orange liqueur)
- ½ ripe banana, peeled
- ½ ounce lime juice
- 1 cup crushed ice
- 4 cherries to decorate

Method

Combine all ingredients in an electric blender except the cherries, and puree for 30 seconds. Serve in a cocktail glass decorated with cherries on cocktail sticks.

Between the Sheets

- -

Ingredients

1½ oz. dark or light rum

½ ounce Triple Sec (orange-flavored liqueur)

½ ounce lemon juice

2 ice cubes

Method

Combine the rum, Triple Sec, and lemon juice. Shake well with the ice cubes; and strain into a cocktail glass. Serves 1.

NOTE: Triple Sec is an orange-flavored liqueur made from the dried peels of bitter oranges from the Caribbean. Triple sec, which is French for Triple Dry, is one-third as sweet as regular Curacao. It is widely used in mixed drinks and recipes as a sweetening and flavoring agent.

Caribbean Sailor's Coffee

. . . .

Ingredients

½ cup of fresh strong coffee
1 ounce brandy
1 oz. Cointreau, or other orange liqueur
1 teaspoon brown sugar
whipped cream
dark chocolate, grated

Variations:

Irish Coffee – substitute the brandy and liqueur for 2 ounces Irish whiskey and increase the sugar to 2 teaspoons.

Kahlua Coffee – substitute the brandy and liqueur for 2 ounces Kahlua.

1 serving

Method

Pour hot coffee into a large wine glass, add sugar and stir to dissolve. Add brandy and liqueur, stir and mix. Float whipped cream on top (to prevent the cream from sinking, pour over back of a spoon). Sprinkle grated chocolate over top and serve immediately.

El Presidente

Ingredients

1½ oz. light rum

¾ ounce dry vermouth

Dash Angostura bitters

2 ice cubes

Method

Combine all the ingredients in a mixing glass and mix well.
Serve in a cocktail glass. Serve 1

Frozen Daiquiri

Ingredients

1½ oz. light rum

1 oz. limejuice

1 teaspoon fine granulated sugar

Crushed ice

Method

Mix the rum, limejuice, and sugar with the crushed ice and blend for 30 seconds.

Pour into a champagne glass and serve with 2 short straws. Serve 1

Hawaiian Raspberry Smoothie

· ·

Ingredients

3 cups fresh or frozen red raspberries (about 12 oz.)

2 bananas, fresh or frozen

¾ cup pineapple juice, unsweetened

¾ cup orange juice

¾ cup ice

1½ cups fat free vanilla yogurt

Pinch of salt

Method

Combine everything in a blender and process until smooth, 1 to 2 minutes, scraping down sides as necessary. Divide among glasses.

TIP: When you have too many bananas on hand, toss them in the freezer (peel to help prevent freezer burn). Bananas keep frozen for months, so you can make creamy smoothies like this one at a moment's notice. Just cut off the peel with knife.

Hot Cocoa

Ingredients

- 2 tablespoons grated cocoa or powdered cocoa
- 2 cups water
- ¼ teaspoon grated nutmeg
- ¼ teaspoon cinnamon
- 1 tablespoon white flour (optional)
- ½ cup milk
- 2 tablespoons sugar

Method

Put two cups of water to boil in a pot. Add two tablespoons of grated cocoa, grated nutmeg, and cinnamon. Allow it to boil for approximately four minutes.

Add milk to the pot. Take ½ cup of water and add flour to thicken to prevent it from making lumps. The flour is optional and its only for if you want it a bit thick. Add sugar for taste.

Jamaican Rumba

· ·

Ingredients

2 inch slice fresh pineapple, skin removed

¼ cup coconut milk

4 tablespoons white rum

1 small banana, peeled

2 teaspoons honey

1¼ cup milk

Crushed ice to serve

Sliced pineapple to decorate

Sliced banana to decorate

Method

Place all the ingredients, except the ice and garnishes, in a blender or food processor and process until smooth. Taste and add extra rum, if desired.

Serve chilled with crushed ice and decorate each glass with sliced banana and pineapple.

Lady Brown Cocktail

Ingredients

2 teaspoons lemon juice

1/2 shot gin (or 2 oz.)

2 teaspoons Curacao

Method

Shake together briefly and then serve over 3 ice cubes in a cocktail glass.

Pawpaw Orange Drink

Ingredients

- 1 ripe pawpaw
- ½ pint orange juice
- Juice of 1 lime
- 2 pints water
- 4 oz. raw cane sugar

Method

Peel the pawpaw, cut it in half. Scoop out and discard the black seeds. Roughly chop the flesh and liquidize in an electric blender until a smooth puree in produced. Mix the pawpaw with the orange juice, limejuice and water. Stir in the raw cane sugar until it is dissolved. Chill.

Serves 4-6

Pineapple Cordial

Ingredients

1 ripe pineapple

4-5 slices peeled root ginger

3 whole cloves

2 limes

2 pints boiling water

4 oz. raw cane sugar

Method

Peel the pineapple thickly and reserve the flesh for use in another dish. Crush the slices of root ginger and thinly slice the limes. Place the pineapple peel, ginger, limes and whole cloves in a large bowl. Pour on the boiling water, cover and allow steeping for 24 hours. Strain the liquid discarding the pineapple peel, limes and spices. Stir in the raw cane sugar until dissolved. Chill.

Serves 4-6

This is an excellent way of using fresh pineapple trimmings. The refreshing ginger flavored drink can be served with ice and garnished with slices of lime

Watermelon Lemonade

. . . .

Be sure to reduce sugar if watermelon is sweet

Ingredients

6 cups 1 inch cubes seedless watermelon

1 cup fresh lemon juice

6 cups water

¾ cup cane sugar

Crushed ice

Mint sprigs for garnish

Method

Working with batches as necessary, puree watermelon and lemon juice in a blender until smooth. Transfer to a large container. Add water and sugar, and stir until dissolved. Pour over ice in tall glasses, garnish with mint and thin slices of watermelon, if desired and serve.

Serves 16

West Coast Cocoa

Ingredients

1/3 cup unsweetened cocoa powder

¼ cup sugar

3 cups milk

2 teaspoons grated orange peel

¼ teaspoon almond extract

4 sticks cinnamon

Method

1. Combine cocoa and sugar in 4 cup glass measure.
2. Add ½ cup milk, and blend to make smooth paste.
3. Stir in remaining 2½ cups milk, orange peel, and almond extract. Stir until sugar is dissolved.
4. Cook in a pan for 7 minutes. Pour in mugs and insert cinnamon sticks.

4 servings

Main Dishes

Baked BBQ Meatballs

Ingredients

3 pounds hamburger, ground round

1 (12 oz.) can evaporated milk

1 cup quick oatmeal

1 cup soda crackers, crumbled

2 eggs

½ cup onions chopped

½ teaspoon garlic powder

2 teaspoons salt

½ teaspoon pepper

2 teaspoons chili powder

1 teaspoon dried parsley

Sauce

2 cups ketchup

½ teaspoon garlic powder

2 cups brown sugar

½ onion chopped

Method

Mix hamburger, milk, oatmeal, eggs, soda crackers, onions, garlic powder, salt, pepper, chili pepper and parsley. Shape into small meatballs. Place in 9x13 baking pan. Cook sauce ingredients until sugar is dissolved. Pour sauce over meatballs and bake 350°F for 1 hour.

Baked Sweet Potato

Ingredients

2 pounds sweet potato

2 oz. unsalted butter or vegetable margarine

Juice of ½ orange

Freshly ground black pepper

2-3 firm tomatoes

Method

1. Carefully wash the sweet potatoes and boil in their skins in plenty of water for 20-25 minutes until soft. Drain.

2. When cool enough to handle, remove the skins and rub the potatoes through a sieve.

3. Mix 1 ounce of butter into the sweet potato puree together with the orange juice. Lightly season with freshly ground black pepper.

4. Butter a shallow baking dish and spread the mixture evenly in it. Top with sliced tomatoes and dot with remaining butter. Bake in a preheated oven at 350 degrees for 20 minutes.

Caribbean Fig Croquette

Ingredients

6 green bananas boiled and mashed
(2 day old bananas work well. The texture is smoother
when you mash them, but they're not sweet)
1 tablespoon butter
1 small onion, finely chopped
2 to 3 cloves of garlic
1 stalk of chive or green onions
1 to 2 sprigs of parsley
½ cup grated cheese (optional)
salt and pepper to taste
olive oil

Method

Mix all ingredients and use 2 tablespoons of mixture to form a cylindrical type shape.

Add about 1/2 inch of olive oil in shallow frying pan and fry until dark brown all over. (Do not deep fry).

Serve with stewed codfish, sweet plantains and cristophene/carrot medley.

Caribbean Rice and Peas

Ingredients

Soak overnight or by quick method:

2 cups dry pigeon peas, pinto beans, or kidney beans

6 cups water

1 teaspoon salt

Bring to a boil, reduce heat, and simmer just until tender—about 40 minutes.

Drain beans, reserving liquid.

Heat in large covered skillet:

2 teaspoons oil or margarine

Add: 1 clove garlic, crushed

2 green onions, chopped

1 large tomato, chopped

1 teaspoon limejuice (optional)

1/8 teaspoon ground cloves

1 teaspoon chopped parsley

¼ **teaspoon pepper**

Drained beans

Sauté about 5 minutes.

Add: 2 cups rice

4 cups reserved bean liquid, (add water if necessary**)**

Method

Bring to a boil, cover, reduce heat to simmer, and cook 20-25 minutes without stirring.

Chicken and Macaroni Salad

· ·

Ingredients

1 cup uncooked elbow macaroni

1 cup diced cucumber

1½ cups cut up cooked chicken

1 tablespoon grated onion

1 teaspoon snipped parsley

½ cup mayonnaise or salad dressing

½ teaspoon salt

¼ teaspoon pepper

4 cups bite size pieces lettuce

Method

1. Cook macaroni as directed on package.
2. Drain and rinse in cold water.
3. Mix all ingredients except lettuce. Cover and refrigerate.
4. Just before serving, toss with lettuce.
5. Garnish with parsley and tomato wedges.

Yield: 4 to 6 servings

Substitutions

For fresh onion: 1 teaspoon instant minced onion.

For fresh parsley: 1 teaspoon parsley flakes.

Chicken Chili

Ingredients

1 tablespoon olive or vegetable oil

1 medium onion, chopped (1/2 cup)

½ cup chopped red bell pepper

1 can (10 3/4 oz.) condensed cream of chicken soup

1¾ cups chicken broth (from 32 oz. carton)

1 cup water

2 cups diced cooked chicken

2 cans (15.5 oz. each) white beans, drained, rinsed

1 can (4.5 oz.) chopped green chiles, undrained

½ teaspoon dried oregano leaves

½ teaspoon ground cumin

½ cup sour cream, if desired

Chopped fresh cilantro, if desired

Method

In 4 quart saucepan, heat oil over medium high heat. Add onion and bell pepper. Cook 2 to 3 minutes, stirring frequently, until tender.

Stir in soup, broth and water. Cook 1 to 2 minutes, stirring frequently, until smooth and well blended. Stir in chicken, beans, chiles, oregano and cumin. Heat to boiling; reduce heat to medium low. Cook uncovered 10 to 15 minutes, stirring occasionally, until thoroughly heated.

Top with sour cream and cilantro.

Cowboy Mashed Potato

. . . .

Ingredients

1 pound red potatoes

1 pound yellow potatoes

1 fresh jalapeno pepper, sliced

12 ounces baby carrots

4 cloves garlic

1 (10 oz.) package frozen white corn, thawed

¼ cup butter

½ cup shredded cheddar cheese

Salt and pepper to taste

Method

1. Place red potatoes, yellow potatoes, and jalapeno pepper, carrots and garlic cloves in a large pot. Cover with water, and bring to a boil over high heat. Cook 15 to 20 minutes, or until potatoes are tender. Drain water from pot.

2. Stir in corn and butter. Mash the mixture with a potato masher until butter is melted and potatoes have reached desired consistency. Mix in cheese, salt, and pepper. Serve hot. Servings: 10

Green Banana With Salt Fish Must Have

. . . .

Ingredients

4 pounds of green bananas

¼ cup of chopped celery

¼ cup chopped parsley

3 cloves of garlic chopped

¼ cup of chopped green peppers

2 pounds salt fish

1 tablespoon of chicken based seasoning

¼ cup vegetable oil

Method

1. Remove skin of the green bananas, cook in a pan of warm water for 15-20 minutes. Add salt and chicken flavored seasoning to the water.

2. Prick bananas with a fork. If soft, bananas are ready. Let the green bananas stand in the pan to cool slightly.

3. Clean salt fish under cold water. Cut into small pieces, and place in a pan to boil for 20 minutes. Remove salt fish from water and place in a container of cold water to remove extra salt. When salt fish is cooled down, shred and place in a bowl.

4. In a medium size frying pan, put ¼ cup vegetable oil and add celery, parsley, onion, garlic and pepper. Sauté in the hot oil and make sure all seasoning is covered. Stir for 4 minutes and add salt to taste if needed, add salt fish to pan.

5. Remove the bananas from the water, put a few chopped ones onto a plate and add some salt fish on top. You can add some cooked vegetables on a side or a small salad. Serve the bananas warm. Enjoy

Green Fig and Salt Fish Pie

Ingredients

2 pounds green figs (bananas)

1 pound saltfish

1/2 pound cheddar cheese

1/2 cup milk

1 tablespoon lime juice

2 sweet peppers

2 tomatoes, thinly sliced

1 onion sliced

1/2 teaspoon black pepper

1 teaspoon bread crumbs

Method

1. Boil the green figs (bananas) until tender. Peel and crush with fork while still hot and sprinkle with limejuice to prevent darkening.
2. Soak the fish in boiling water to remove most of the salt and soak it in cold water to remove additional salt. Remove the skin and bones; shred fish.
3. Press half of the crushed fig (bananas) in a greased baking pie dish. Sprinkle 1/2 of shredded fish on fig. Spread half of sweet peppers (cut into thin strips) onion, tomatoes, cheese and black pepper.
4. Repeat layer - beginning with green fig and ending with grated cheese and black pepper.
5. Top with milk and sprinkle with breadcrumbs. Bake in an oven at 350 degrees oven for 30-40 minutes or until the cheese has melted and is golden brown.

Hopping John

· ·

Ingredients

1 ¼ cup black eye peas, rinsed and soaked overnight

1 tablespoon vegetable oil

½ yellow onion, chopped

1 celery stalk, including leaves finely chopped

5 cups water or chicken stock

salt and ground pepper to taste

½ cup long grain white rice

Tabasco sauce, or other hot-pepper sauce

Chopped parsley

Method

Soak black eye peas overnight in water to cover by several inches. In a heavy saucepan warm the oil. Add the onion celery and sauté just to heat, about one minute. Stir in water or stock and bring to a boil. Add the drained black eye peas, reduce the heat to medium, cover partially and cook, stirring occasionally until tender 40-50 minutes. Season to taste with salt and pepper.

Stir in rice and continue cooking until the rice is tender about 15 minutes. Season with hot pepper sauce and sprinkle with chopped parsley. Serves 6

Black eye peas and rice has been known for generations. It might have gotten its name from South Carolina or in New Orleans, or because you feel so good from eating it you could just hop around. It's one way southerners eat black eye peas on New Year's day, a custom believed to guarantee good luck the rest of the year.

Jiffy Hot Dish

Ingredients

- 1 pound ground beef or ground round
- 1 ¼ cup uncooked macaroni rings
- 1 can cream style corn
- 1 can chicken rice soup undiluted

Method

Cook ground beef in skillet until pink color is not visible but cooked. Mix all the other ingredients together and bake in covered casserole at 350° degrees for 1 hour or until brown.

Macaroni and Cheese Baked

. . . .

Ingredients

1 1/2 cups uncooked elbow macaroni

5 tablespoons butter - divided

3 tablespoons all-purpose flour

1 1/2 cups milk

1 cup (4 oz.) shredded sharp cheddar cheese

2 oz. velveeta cheese, cubed

1/2 teaspoon salt

1/4 teaspoon pepper

2 tablespoons dry breadcrumbs

Method

1. Cook macaroni according to package directions: Drain and place in a greased 1-1/2 quart baking dish.

2. In a saucepan, melt 4 tablespoons of the butter over medium heat. Stir in flour until smooth. Gradually add milk, continuing to stir, bring to a boil. Cook and stir for 2 minutes. Reduce heat.

3. Stir in cheeses, salt/pepper until cheese is melted. Pour over macaroni; mix well. Melt the remaining butter; add the breadcrumbs. Sprinkle over casserole.

Bake uncovered 375°F for 30 minutes.

Macaroni Salad

....

Ingredients

8 oz. dried elbow macaroni (2 cups)

½ pound green beans cut into 1inch pieces

¼ cup lemon juice

1 tablespoon Dijon style mustard

1 teaspoon salt

¼ teaspoon freshly ground black pepper

1/3 cup olive oil

1/3 cup plain yogurt or dairy sour cream

5 oz. cubed cheddar cheese (1-1/4 cups)

1 cup fresh spinach leaves

1 large tomato, seeded and chopped (1 cup)

½ cup chopped green onions

1 tablespoon snipped fresh tarragon or crumbled dried tarragon

Method

1. Cook macaroni according to package directions.
2. Cook green beans during last 5 minutes of cooking. Drain. Rinse with cold water; drain well.
3. In a medium bowl, whisk together lemon juice, mustard, salt, and pepper. Whisk in olive oil until thickened. Whisk in yogurt.
4. Add cheese, spinach, tomato, onions, and tarragon to macaroni. Add dressing; toss. Serve immediately or cover and refrigerate 2 to 24 hours.

One Pot Spaghetti

. . . .

Ingredients

8 oz. ground beef

1 cup sliced fresh mushrooms or

6 oz. jar sliced mushrooms drained

½ cup chopped onion (1 medium)

1 clove garlic, minced

1 14-oz. can chicken broth or beef broth

1-3/4 cups water

1 6-oz. can tomato paste

1 teaspoon dried Italian seasoning

¼ teaspoon black pepper

6 oz. dried spaghetti, broken

¼ cup grated Parmesan cheese

Method

In a large saucepan, cook the ground beef, fresh mushrooms, onion and garlic until meat is brown and onion is tender. Drain.

Stir in the canned mushrooms, broth, water, tomato paste, Italian seasoning, and pepper. Bring to boiling. Add the broken spaghetti, a little at a time, stirring constantly. Return to boiling, and reduce heat. Boil gently, uncovered, for 20 minutes or until spaghetti is tender and sauce is the desired consistency, stirring frequently. Serve with Parmesan cheese. Makes 4 servings.

Pasta With Shrimp

· ·

Ingredients

8 oz. fresh or frozen shrimp shells

8 thin stalks asparagus

½ of a 9 oz. package refrigerated angel hair pasta

1 teaspoon olive oil

2 cloves garlic, minced

3 medium plum tomatoes, seeded and coarsely chopped

2 tablespoons dry white wine

1/8 teaspoon black pepper

2 teaspoons butter or margarine

2 tablespoons finely shredded fresh basil

Method

1. Thaw shrimp; if frozen. Peel and devein shrimp. Rinse shrimp and pat dry with paper towels. Set aside.

2. Trim ends off asparagus. Slice the stalks into 1-1/2-inch pieces. Set aside. Cook pasta according to package directions; drain. Return pasta to saucepan; cover and keep warm.

3. In a medium skillet heat oil over medium heat. Add garlic; cook and stir for 10 seconds. Add tomatoes; cook and stir for 2 minutes.

4. Add the asparagus, wine, salt, and black pepper. Cook, uncovered, for 3 minutes. Stir in shrimp. Cook, uncovered, for 2 to 5 minute more or until shrimp are opaque. Stir in butter until melted.

5. Add the shrimp mixture and basil to pasta; toss gently to coat.

Makes 2 servings

Pigeon Peas and Rice

Ingredients

2 cups long grain rice

4 tablespoons butter

1 quart water

1 onion, chopped

1 sprig celery

sprig thyme

1 clove garlic

2 cups shelled pigeon peas (fresh)

¼ pound cooking ham (cubed)

2 tablespoons tomato sauce

Method

1. Melt 2 tablespoons butter in a saucepan on medium heat. Add chopped onion, pigeon peas and cubed ham. Cook until brown.
2. Add celery, thyme, garlic, and continue to cook for 15 minutes.
3. Add uncooked rice, water, tomato sauce, and bring to a boil. Cover and reduce heat and cook for 35 minutes or until liquid is absorbed.
4. Add the remainder of the butter to the cooked rice.

Serves 4

Rice and Beans

Ingredients

1 cup kidney beans

2 fresh thyme sprigs

2 ounce piece of creamed coconut or ½ cup coconut cream

2 bay leaves

1 onion finely chopped

2 garlic cloves, crushed

½ teaspoon ground allspice

1 red or green bell pepper seeded and chopped

2½ cup water

2½ cups long grain rice

Salt and ground black pepper

Method

1. Put the red kidney beans in a large bowl. Pour in enough cold water to cover the beans generously. Cover the bowl and leave the beans to soak overnight.
2. Drain the beans and tip them into a large pan with a tight fitting lid. Pour in enough water to cover the beans. Bring to boil and boil for 10 minutes, then lower the heat and simmer for 1½ hours or until the beans are tender.
3. Add the thyme, creamed coconut or coconut cream, bay leaves, onion, garlic, allspice and pepper. Season and stir in the measured water.
4. Bring to a boil and add the rice. Stir well, reduce the heat and cover the pan. Simmer for 25-30 minutes, until all the liquid has been absorbed. Serve as an accompaniment to fish, meat or vegetarian dishes.

Shepherd's Pie

Ingredients

1½ ground round beef

1 onion chopped

2 cups vegetables – chopped carrots, corn, peas

2 pounds potatoes

8 tablespoons butter (1 stick)

½ cup beef broth

1 teaspoon Worcestershire sauce

Salt, pepper, other seasonings

Method

1. Peel and cut potatoes in quarters, and boil in salted water until tender.
2. As potatoes are cooking, melt 4 tablespoons butter (1/2 stick) in a large frying pan.
3. Sauté onion in butter until tender over medium heat. Add the vegetables according to cooking time. Add carrots and corn after the meat has been cooked.
4. Add ground beef and sauté until no longer pink. Add salt and pepper, Worcestershire sauce. Add half a cup of beef broth and cook uncovered over low heat for 10 minutes, adding more beef broth as necessary to keep moist.
5. Mash potatoes and add the remaining butter, season to taste.
6. Place beef and onion in baking dish. Spread the mashed potatoes on top and rough up with a fork to make peaks, or make some designs in the potatoes.
7. Bake in a 400° degrees oven until bubbling and brown for 30 minutes. Broil for the last 5 minutes.

NOTE: Shepherd Pie is an English casserole dish, made with lamb or mutton. Americans make Shepherd's Pie with beef.

Vegetable Lasagna

Ingredients

½ package 8 oz. lasagna noodles, uncooked

8 oz. sliced fresh mushrooms

¾ cup chopped green bell pepper

½ cup chopped onion

2 cloves garlic chopped

2 teaspoons olive or vegetable oil

1 (26 oz.) jar pasta sauce

1 teaspoon basil leaves

1 teaspoon oregano leaves

1 (15 oz.) container ricotta cheese

3 cups (12 oz.) shredded mozzarella cheese

2 eggs

½ cup Parmesan cheese

Method

1. Cook lasagna as package directs. Preheat oven to 350°F.
2. In a large saucepan, over medium heat, cook mushrooms, green pepper, onion and garlic in oil until tender.
3. Stir in pasta sauce, basil and oregano. Bring to a boil; reduce heat and simmer 15 minutes.
4. Combine ricotta cheese, 2 cups mozzarella and eggs; mix well. Spread ½ cup sauce on bottom of greased 13X9 inch baking dish.
5. Top with half of the lasagna, ricotta cheese mixture, sauce, and Parmesan cheese. Repeat layering.
6. Top with remaining 1 cup mozzarella. Cover and bake 45 to 50 minutes or until hot and bubbly.
7. Uncover. Let stand 15 minutes. Garnish if desired. Refrigerate leftovers.

Winter Vegetable Stew

Ingredients

1 cup onion, cut into ½ inch wedges

1 sweet potato, diced

2 carrots, diced

1 pound banana or butternut squash, cut in squares

1 cup parsnips, diced

2 cloves garlic, minced

1 red bell pepper, strips

2 cups low sodium, low fat vegetable broth

1 cup pureed tomato

2 tablespoons limejuice

¼ teaspoon cayenne pepper

1 (10 oz.) package frozen peas

¼ teaspoon salt

1/8 teaspoon black pepper

1 bunch cilantro sprigs, rinsed or thinly sliced green onions

Method

1. Peel and cut the sweet potato, carrot, squash, and parsnips into ¾ inch pieces.
2. Mince or press garlic.
3. Cut bell pepper into ½ inch strips.
4. Cook onions, sweet potato, carrots, squash, parsnips, garlic, and 1 cup of vegetable broth in a covered pan for 10 minutes, stir occasionally. Add water if mixture sticks to pan. Add 1 more cup of broth, bell pepper, tomato sauce, lime juice, and cayenne pepper to taste. Return to a boil and reduce heat.
5. Simmer covered until vegetables are tender. Add broth as needed.
6. Add peas and stir occasionally until hot. Add salt and pepper to taste. Ladle into soup bowls, and garnish with cilantro or sliced green onions.

Makes 6 servings

Meat and Poultry

Baked Cornish Hens with Vegetables

Ingredients

2 Cornish hens, split lengthwise

3 tablespoons lemon juice

3 tablespoons olive oil

1 clove pressed garlic

2 tablespoons dry rosemary

4 shallots, unpeeled

6 baby carrots

Red skinned potatoes, slice 1/4 inch thick

Method

Place hens skin side up, in a roasting pan. Mix lemon juice, oil, rosemary and garlic. Pour over hens. Cut shallots in half lengthwise.

Bake hens uncovered 450° degrees for 45 minutes or until done.

Barbecued Spareribs

Ingredients

3 to 4 pounds spareribs

3 small onions, sliced

2 tablespoons vinegar

2 tablespoons Worcestershire sauce

1 tablespoon salt

1 teaspoon paprika

½ teaspoon red pepper

1 teaspoon chili powder

¾ cup catsup

¾ cup water

Method

Cut meaty spareribs into servings. Sprinkle with salt and pepper. Place in a roaster pan and cover with onions. Combine remaining ingredients and pour over meat. Cover and bake in 350 degrees oven for 1½ hours. Baste occasionally, turning spareribs once or twice. Remove cover from roaster during the last 15 minutes of baking to brown spareribs.

Buffalo Chicken Hot Wings

. . . .

Ingredients

20 chicken wings, split and tips removed

3 tablespoons butter melted

½ cup red pepper sauce

¾ cup tomato sauce

1½ tablespoon chili powder

1 teaspoons cayenne pepper

1 teaspoon garlic

½ teaspoon black pepper

2 teaspoons vinegar

1 teaspoon sugar

1 teaspoon ground cinnamon

Blue Cheese Dip

½ cup sour cream

½ cup crumbled blue cheese

½ cup mayonnaise

1 teaspoon white wine vinegar

1 clove garlic

Mix all ingredients together to make dip. Enjoy!

Method

1. Preheat oven to 375 degrees F.
2. Bake wings in preheated oven for 35 minutes, or until cooked through and crispy.
3. In a small bowl, combine melted butter, red pepper sauce, tomato sauce, chili powder, cayenne pepper, garlic, black pepper, vinegar, sugar, and ground cinnamon. Mix together to make sauce.
4. When wings are baked, dip in sauce to coat well, shake off any excess and return coated wings to the baking sheet. Reduce oven temperature to 300 degrees F and bake for another 30 minutes to set sauce.

Chicken/Turkey Broccoli Rice Casserole

Ingredients

1 (10 oz.) package frozen cut broccoli

1 cup cooked rice

½ cup onion, chopped

6 oz. (1 cup) cooked chicken or turkey breast, diced

1 (10 ½ oz.) cream of chicken soup

¼ teaspoon lemon pepper

Method

Preheat oven to 350°. Spray an 8 x 8 inch baking pan with nonstick cooking spray.
In medium saucepan, cook broccoli in a small amount of water until tender. Drain. In a large bowl, combine cooked broccoli, rice, onion and chicken/turkey. Add soup and lemon pepper. Mix gently to combine. Pour mixture into prepared pan and bake uncovered for 45 minutes.

Yield: 4 servings

Chicken Stroganoff

Ingredients

2 pounds skinless, boneless chicken breast halves and/or thighs

1 cup chopped onion

2 10 ¾-oz. cans condensed cream of mushroom soup with roasted garlic

1/3 cup water

12 oz. dried wide egg noodles

1 (8 oz.) carton dairy sour cream

Freshly ground black pepper

Method

1. Cut chicken into 1-inch pieces. In a 4-quart slow cooker combine the chicken pieces and onion. In a medium bowl stir together the soup and water. Pour over chicken and onion.
2. Cover and cook on low-heat setting for 6 to 7 hours or on high-heat setting for 3 to 3-1/2 hours.
3. Cook noodles according to package directions. Drain. Just before serving, stir sour cream into mixture in cooker. To serve, spoon stroganoff mixture over hot cooked noodles. If desired, sprinkle with black pepper. Makes 6 to 8 servings.

Chicken With Black Beans and Rice

Ingredients

¼ cup all purpose flour

1½ teaspoon chili powder

¼ teaspoon salt

1/4 teaspoon black pepper

2 ¼ to 3 pounds chicken parts
(Breast halves, thigh, wings, and drumsticks)

2 tablespoons cooking oil

1 15-oz. can black beans, rinsed and drained

1 14.5-oz. diced tomatoes with onion and green pepper, undrained

1 cup tomato juice

1 cup frozen whole kernel corn

2/3 cup long grain uncooked rice

1/8-1/4 teaspoon cayenne pepper

2 cloves garlic, minced

Method

1. In a large plastic bag combine flour, 1 teaspoon of the chili powder, the salt, and pepper. Add chicken pieces in a sealed bag; shake to coat.

2. In a very large skillet brown chicken on all sides in hot oil over medium heat about 10 minutes, turning occasionally. Remove chicken from skillet and set aside to discard drippings. Add black beans, undrained tomatoes, tomato juice, corn, uncooked rice, the remaining ½ teaspoon chili powder, the cayenne pepper, and garlic to the skillet. Bring to boiling. Transfer rice mixture to a 13x9x2 inch baking dish or 3 quart rectangular casserole. Arrange chicken pieces on top of rice mixture.

3. Bake, covered, in a 375° degrees for 45 to 50 minutes or until chicken is cooked and rice is tender. Makes 6 servings.

Chicken With Capers

. . . .

Ingredients

4 skinless, boneless, chicken breast

1 teaspoon mustard

¼ cup seasoned dry bread crumbs

Salt and pepper to taste

8 oz. green beans, trimmed

2 lemons, 1 sliced and 1 juice

1 teaspoon capers

6 tablespoon olive oil

Method

1. Place one chicken breast between sheets of plastic wrap. Lightly pound with flat side of meat mallet and repeat.

2. Brush chicken with mustard; sprinkle with salt, pepper, and breadcrumbs to coat.

3. Heat 2 tablespoons olive oil in skillet over medium heat. Add chicken. Cook 4 minutes per side or until no pink remains. Transfer to plates.

4. Add 2 tablespoons olive oil to skillet. Cook green beans in olive oil for 4 minutes or until crisp tender; add lemon slices and juice of one lemon the last minute. Transfer to plates. Add juice and capers to skillet; heat through. Drizzle on chicken.

Makes 4 servings

Chicken with Rice and Pigeon Peas

. . . .

Ingredients

1 onion chopped

2 garlic cloves

1 tablespoon chopped fresh chives

1 tablespoon chopped thyme

2 celery sticks with leaves, chopped

4 tablespoons water

Fresh coconut meat from ½ coconut chopped

Liquid from fresh coconut

16 oz. can pigeon peas, drained

1 fresh chili pepper, 1 tsp salt

Freshly ground black pepper

2 tablespoons vegetable oil, 2 tablespoons sugar

3 ½ pounds chicken, chopped

1 pound uncooked rice, rinsed and drained

1¼ cup water

Method

1. Put the onion, garlic, chives, thyme, celery, and 4 tablespoons water in a blender or food processor and process together. Put all of the mixture into large saucepan.
2. Make coconut milk using the coconut meat and liquid.
3. Add the coconut milk to the pan with the pigeon peas and chili pepper. Cook over low heat for 15 minutes, and season with salt and freshly ground black pepper.
4. Heat the oil in flameproof casserole. Add the sugar and heat until it begins to caramelize.
5. Add the raw chicken to the casserole and cook for 15 minutes until it has browned. Stir in the pigeon pea mixture, rice, and water. Bring to the boil, then reduce the heat, cover, and simmer for 20 minutes, or until the rice and chicken are cooked. Discard the chili pepper before serving. Serves 6.

Chili Chicken and Pasta

Ingredients

6 oz. dried angel hair pasta

3 fresh ears of sweet corn

¼ cup olive or cooking oil

4 small skinless boneless chicken breast halves

1 ½ teaspoon chili powder

¼ teaspoon salt

¼ teaspoon pepper

2 medium tomatoes, sliced

3 tablespoons lime or lemon juice

Lime halves and snipped fresh parsley (optional)

Method

1. Cook pasta and corn in lightly salted boiling water according to pasta package directions. Drain and rinse with cold water until cool.

2. Sprinkle with one teaspoon chili powder, the salt, and pepper. In a large skillet cook chicken in one-tablespoon hot oil over medium heat for 8 to 10 minutes turning once.

3. Combine remaining oil, chili powder and the limejuice; shake well to combine. Cut corn from cob.

4. Divide chicken, corn, tomatoes and pasta on four dinner plates. Drizzle with dressing and sprinkle lightly with salt and pepper. Serve with lime and parsley.

Chinese Style Chicken

· ·

Ingredients

1 tablespoon olive or canola oil

¼ pound boneless, skinless chicken breasts, cut into ¼ inch strips

2 large carrots, sliced

1 cup snow peas

1 small red pepper, cut into strips

2 green onions, cut into ½ inch pieces

2 cloves garlic, minced

4 teaspoons cornstarch

½ teaspoon ground ginger

1 cup chicken broth

3 tablespoons reduced sodium soy sauce

1 ½ cup instant brown rice, uncooked

Method

Heat oil in large skillet. Add chicken, vegetables and garlic; stir fry until chicken is tender and cooked through. Mix cornstarch, ginger, broth, and soy sauce until smooth. Add to skillet. Stirring constantly, bring to boil for one minute. Meanwhile, prepare 4 servings of rice as directed on package, omitting margarine and salt. Serve chicken mixture over rice. 4 servings

Crock-Pot Apple Chicken Stew

· ·

Fall is a perfect time to dust off the crock-pot and make healthy recipes for your family.

Ingredients

4 medium potatoes, cubed

4 medium carrots, cut into ¼ inch slices

1 medium red onion, halved and sliced

1 celery rib, thinly sliced

¾ teaspoon dried thyme

pepper to taste

½ teaspoon caraway seed

2 pounds boneless skinless chicken breasts, cubed

1 tablespoon olive oil

2-4 large tart apples, peeled and cubed

1 ¼ cups apple cider

1 tablespoon cider vinegar

1 bay leaf

Method

In a slow cooker, layer potatoes, carrots, onion and celery.

Combine thyme, pepper and caraway; sprinkle half over vegetables.

In a skillet, sauté chicken cubes in oil, until browned. Transfer to a slow cooker

Top with apple. Combine the apple cider and vinegar. Pour over chicken and apple

Sprinkle with remaining salt mixture. Top with bay leaf.

Cover and cook on high for 4-5 hours, or until vegetables are tender and chicken is cooked.

Remove the bay leaf. Stir before serving. Serves 6.

Curried Goat or Lamb

. . . .

Ingredients

2 tablespoons oil

1½ pounds goat or lamb, cut into small cubes

3 large onions, diced

2 tablespoons curry powder

2 large potatoes, diced

2 ripe tomatoes, diced

3 cups chicken stock

1 tablespoon wine vinegar

½ teaspoon salt

1 teaspoon paprika

1 bay leaf

Method

1. Heat the oil in a large pot or Dutch oven over medium heat, and brown the meat. Remove the meat with a spoon and put aside. Sauté the onions and garlic in the drippings until soft but not brown, about 5 minutes.

2. Stir in curry powder and potatoes, and cook for about 3 minutes to release the curry flavor.

3. Add the tomato, stock, vinegar, salt and paprika. Return the meat to the pan, cover and simmer for 1½ hour. Add ½ cup water if the mixture becomes too dry. Add the bay leaf and cook for 30 minutes more until the meat is tender. Remove the bay leaf and serve with plain rice or rice and peas.

Fried Chicken

Ingredients

Before frying, the chicken is soaked in water or buttermilk to keep it moist

1 chicken, 3-4 pounds, cut into serving pieces, or 3-4 pounds chicken parts

For buttermilk fried chicken:

1½ cups buttermilk, 1 egg

For southern fried chicken:

Large bowl of ice water

For coating:

1 cup all purpose flour

½ teaspoon sugar

1 teaspoon salt

½ teaspoon ground black pepper

½ teaspoon garlic powder

1 teaspoon paprika

¼ teaspoon cayenne pepper

2½ cups vegetable shortening, lard, or peanut or vegetable oil

Method

If making the buttermilk fried chicken, place the chicken pieces in a bowl with 1 cup of the buttermilk. Cover and refrigerate overnight. Next day, in a bowl, beat the egg and then beat in the remaining ½ cup buttermilk. One piece at a time, retrieve the chicken from the buttermilk dip in the flour mixture; dip in egg mixture, and dip again in the flour mixture. Set on a baking sheet. When all chicken is coated, place in the refrigerator for 15 minutes.

If making the southern fried chicken, soak the chicken pieces in ice water for 15 minutes. Retrieve the chicken pieces one at a time, from the ice water and drop into a bag with coating seasoning. Close and shake well to coat all over. Remove and set on a baking sheet. When all the chicken is coated, place in the refrigerator for at least 15 minutes.

To fry both the southern and buttermilk versions, melt the shortening in a deep fryer or deep heavy pan or high heat to 325-350 degrees fast. Fry the chicken a few pieces at a time turning frequently, until golden and cooked through, 15-20 minutes or fry in hot oil until the juices comes out clear and finish cooking in the oven at 375 degrees for 35 minutes to reduce the amount of oil absorption.

. . . .

Ingredients

1 bone-in ham, 5-8 pounds, ready to cook

6-8 whole cloves

1 cup firmly packed brown sugar

¾ cup honey

1 heaping tablespoon dry mustard

Method

Preheat oven 325 degrees F.

Place the ham in a roasting pan.

Cut diagonal slashes over the surface of the ham and stud with the cloves. In a small bowl, combine the sugar, honey, and mustard and mix well. Using a spoon or pastry brush, spread the mixture all over the surface of the ham, and place the ham in the oven.

Bake, basting frequently with the glaze until it is dark and sticks to the ham. Plan on 20 minutes per pound.

Transfer to a platter, let cool slightly, and then slice and serve with the pan juices on the side.

Grilled Caribbean Chicken

· ·

Ingredients

½ cup lemon juice

1/3 cup honey

3 tablespoons canola oil

6 green onions, sliced

3 jalapeno peppers, seeded and chopped

3 teaspoons dried thyme

¾ teaspoon salt

¼ teaspoon ground allspice

¼ teaspoon ground nutmeg

6 boneless skinless chicken breast halves
(1-1/2 pounds)

Method

1. Place the first nine ingredients in a blender or food processor; cover and process until smooth.
2. Pour ½ cup into a small bowl for basting; cover and refrigerate.
3. Pour remaining marinade into a large resealable plastic bag; add chicken. Seal bag and turn to coat; refrigerate for up to six hours.
4. Drain and discard marinade. Coat grill rack with nonstick cooking spray before starting the grill. Grill chicken, covered, over medium heat for 4-6 minutes on each side or until juices run clear, basting frequently with the reserved marinade. Yield: 6 servings.

NOTE: When cutting or seeding hot peppers, use rubber or plastic gloves to protect your hands. Avoid touching your face.

Grilled Fish, Chicken or Meat

Ingredients

1½ pounds lean beef, cut into 1 inch cubes

1 yellow onion, cut into 1 inch squares

1 fresh red or green chile, minced

2 cloves garlic, minced

½ cup fresh lemon or limejuice

2 tablespoons vegetable oil

Salt and ground black pepper

Tomato Onion relish

Method

Combine the meat cubes and onion squares in a single layer in a ceramic or glass dish. In a small bowl, stir together the chile, garlic, lemon juice, oil and salt and pepper to taste. Pour over the meat and mix well. Let stand at least 1 hour at room temperature, or cover and refrigerate overnight.

Soak bamboo skewers in water to cover. Prepare a charcoal fire. Remove the meat from the marinade and reserve the marinade. Drain the skewers and alternately thread the meat and onions onto the skewers. Grill, turning occasionally, over the hot coals until done, 6-8 minutes.

Meanwhile, in a small saucepan, heat the reserved marinade and boil for 2 minutes. Serve with the cooked meat. Pass the relish.

Serves 4 or 5

Jamaican Jerk Chicken

. . . .

Ingredients

1 tablespoon ground allspice

1 tablespoon dried thyme

1½ teaspoons cayenne pepper

1½ teaspoons black pepper

1½ teaspoons ground sage

¾ teaspoon ground nutmeg

¾ teaspoon cinnamon

2 teaspoons salt

2 teaspoons garlic powder

1 tablespoon sugar

¼ cup olive oil

¼ cup soy sauce

¾ cup white vinegar

½ cup orange juice

Juice of 1 lime

1 Scotch Bonnet pepper, seeded and finely chopped

1 cup chopped white onion

3 green onions, finely chopped

4 chicken breasts (6 to 8 oz.) trimmed of fat

Method

1. In a large bowl, combine the allspice, thyme, cayenne pepper, black pepper, sage, nutmeg, cinnamon, salt, garlic powder and sugar.

2. With a wire whisk, slowly add the olive oil, soy sauce, white vinegar, orange juice, and lime juice.

3. Add the scotch bonnet pepper, onion, and green onions and mix well. Add the chicken breasts, cover and marinade for at least one hour, longer if possible.

4. Preheat an outdoor grill. Remove the breasts from the marinade and grill for 6 minutes on each side or until fully cooked. While grilling, baste with the marinade.

Jamaican Pork Stir-Fry

Jamaican jerk seasoning added to pork and vegetables brings a touch of the Caribbean to your table. Stir frying is a quick cooking method that uses a wok to cook over a high heat. The vegetables are cooked to crisp tender and the meat is cut thin in order for it to cook quickly as well. Prepare this low-fat dish in less than 30 minutes.

Ingredients

2 tablespoons cooking oil

1 16-oz. package frozen stir fry vegetables (carrots, snow peas, mushrooms, and onions)

12 oz. pork strips for stir frying

2 to 3 teaspoons Jamaican jerk seasoning

¾ cup bottled plum sauce

2 cups hot cooked rice or pasta

Chopped peanuts

Method

1. In a wok or large skillet heat oil over medium high heat. Add frozen vegetables; cook and stir for 5 to 7 minutes or until vegetables are crisp-tender and ready to transfer.

2. Toss pork strips with Jamaican jerk seasoning; add the pork strips to the wok. (Add more oil if necessary). Cook and stir for 20 to 25 minutes or until pork is no longer pink but tender.

3. Add the plum sauce to the wok. Return vegetables to the wok. Gently toss all ingredients together to coat. Heat through. Serve over rice. Sprinkle with peanuts.

Makes 4 servings

Jerk Chicken Drumettes

Ingredients

3-4 pounds chicken drumettes

1 tablespoon granulated dried onion

1 tablespoon ground allspice

1 tablespoon ground ginger

1 tablespoon ground thyme

1 teaspoon salt

1-3 teaspoons cayenne pepper

½ teaspoon ground black pepper

1 teaspoon sugar

Dash of ground cinnamon

3 tablespoons garlic powder, or 3 garlic cloves, minced

2-3 tablespoon vegetable oil

¼ cup fresh limejuice, rum, coconut milk, or water

Method

Combine all the dry ingredients and mix well. Store in an airtight container. When ready to use, take a couple tablespoons out for each pound of meat, chicken, or fish and mix with the oil and the liquid of choice. Marinate fish 1 hour and anything else overnight.

Oven Barbecued Chicken

Ingredients

2½ to 3 pounds meaty chicken pieces
(Breast halves, thighs, and drumsticks)

½ cup chopped onion (1 medium)

1 clove garlic, minced

1 tablespoon cooking oil

¾ cup bottled chili sauce

2 tablespoons honey

2 tablespoons soy sauce

1 tablespoon prepared mustard

½ teaspoon prepared horseradish

¼ teaspoon crushed red pepper

Method

1. Skin chicken. Arrange chicken, bone side up, in a 15x10x1 inch baking pan. Bake in a 375 degree F oven for 25 minutes.

2. Meanwhile, for sauce, in a small saucepan cook onion and garlic in hot cooking oil over medium heat until tender but not brown. Stir in chili sauce, honey, soy sauce, mustard, horseradish, and crushed red pepper; heat through.

3. Turn chicken bone side down. Brush half of the sauce over the chicken. Bake for 20 to 30 minutes more or until chicken is no longer pink. Reheat remaining sauce; pass with the chicken. Makes 6 servings.

Oxtail or Short Rib Stew

. . . .

Ingredients

3 tablespoons vegetable oil

3 pounds oxtails, cut into 1½ inch section, or 3 pounds of short ribs

1 yellow onion, finely chopped

3 garlic cloves, chopped

2 large or 4 small bay leaves

½ teaspoon grated nutmeg

1 tablespoon fresh lemon juice, red wine or wine vinegar

2 cans 16 oz. peeled tomatoes with their juice

2 celery stalks, including leaves, finely chopped

½ green bell pepper, seeded and finely chopped

Salt and ground black pepper

Method

In a heavy pot, heat oil over high heat and brown the meat well on all sides. Add all the remaining ingredients except the celery, bell pepper, and salt and pepper. Cover, reduce the heat to medium, and cook until tender, 1½ - 2 hours.

When the meat is tender and beginning to pull away from the bones and the sauce is cooked down, add the celery and bell pepper and season to taste with salt and pepper. Cook 10 minutes longer. This brief cooking ensures a crunch at the end. Serve hot.

Serves 4 to 6

NOTE: This dish can also be cooked in a pressure cooker. It will take roughly 40 minutes.

Roast Chicken with Raisin Corn Bread Stuffing

Ingredients

½ cup celery, finely chopped

½ cup chopped onion

¼ cup chicken broth

3 tablespoons oil

¼ cup raisins

¼ teaspoon dill weed

¼ teaspoon salt

2 cups coarsely crumbled corn bread

1 egg slightly beaten

Chicken broth

1 3-pound whole roasting chicken

Paprika for coloring

Method

In a small saucepan simmer celery and onion in the 3 tablespoons oil. Add ¼ cup chicken broth until tender. In a mixing bowl combine undrained celery mixture, raisins, dill weed, and salt.

1. Add corn bread and beaten egg; toss gently until mixed. Drizzle with desired amount of additional broth to moisten; toss gently to mix.

2. Loosely spoon stuffing mixture into chicken body cavity. Pull neck skin to back; fasten with a small skewer. Slip drumsticks under band of skin to secure or tie the drumsticks securely to tail. Twist wing tips under the back. Place chicken, breast side up, on a rack in a shallow roasting pan. Sprinkle with paprika.

3. Roast, uncovered, in a 375 degree oven for 1-1/4 to 1-1/2 hours or until drumsticks move easily in their sockets and the thickest part feels soft when pressed or until the meat is no longer pink. If using a meat thermometer, it should register 180 degrees F to 185 degrees F when placed in the center of the thigh.

4. When chicken is done, remove it from the oven and cover with aluminum foil. Let stand for 15 to 20 minutes before carving. Remove skin before serving. Garnish with fresh herbs, if desired. Makes 4 servings.

5. **Tip: Bake any of this herbed and slightly sweet stuffing that won't fit in the bird separately in a covered casserole for the last 30 to 45 minutes of chicken roasting time.**

6. **Make-Ahead Tip: Prepare and bake the corn bread. Cover and store at room temperature up to 1 day ahead.**

Slow Cooker Italian Smothered Steak

Ingredients

2 pounds beef boneless round steak

½ teaspoon seasoned salt

¼ teaspoon pepper

1 medium onion, sliced

1 jar (26 oz.) tomato pasta sauce (any variety)

1 package (9 oz.) refrigerated cheese filled tortellini

1 medium zucchini, cut lengthwise in half, Cut crosswise into slices (about 1 cup)

Method

1. Cut beef into 6 serving size pieces; sprinkle with seasoned salt and pepper.
2. Layer beef and onion in 3- to 4 quart slow cooker. Pour pasta sauce over top.
3. Cover and cook on low heat setting 8 to 9 hours.
4. About 20 minutes before serving, stir in tortellini and zucchini. Increase heat setting to high.
5. Cover and cook 15 to 20 minutes or until tortellini are tender.

You can use yellow summer squash instead of the zucchini.

Cut the beef into pieces of same size so that it cooks to the same tenderness.

Fresh baked soft breadsticks and Caesar salad in a bag carry out the Italian theme of this meal.

Slow Cooker Pot Roast and Vegetables

. . . .

Ingredients

4 medium potatoes, peeled, each cut into 6 pieces

4 large carrots, cut into 1-inch pieces

1 large onion, thinly sliced

1 dried bay leaf

1-tablespoon all-purpose flour

1/2-teaspoon salt

1/8-teaspoon pepper

1 beef top round steak, 1/2 inch thick (1-1/2 pound),
Cut into 4 serving pieces

1 3/4 cups beef flavored broth (from 32 oz. carton)

1 teaspoon Worcestershire sauce

2 tablespoons cornstarch

Method

Spray slow cooker with cooking spray and place potatoes, carrots, onion and bay leaf at bottom of slow cooker.

In shallow bowl, mix flour, salt and pepper. Add beef pieces; turn to coat both sides. Spray 12 inch skillet with cooking spray; heat over medium high heat. Add beef and brown on all sides; place in slow cooker. In small bowl, mix 1- 1/2 cups of the broth and the Worcestershire sauce. Pour over beef.

Cover; cook on low heat setting 8 to 10 hours.

With a spoon, remove beef and vegetables to serving platter; cover to keep warm. Pour liquid from slow cooker into 2 quart saucepan; discard bay leaf. In small bowl, mix remaining ¼ cup broth and the cornstarch until smooth; add to liquid in saucepan. Heat to boiling over medium high heat, stirring constantly. Boil 1 minute. Serve sauce with beef and vegetables.

Slow Cooker Rustic Italian Chicken

Ingredients

12 boneless skinless chicken thighs (about 2 pounds)

2 large carrots, cut into 1/2-inch slices

1 medium red bell pepper, chopped (1 cup)

1 cup sliced fresh mushrooms (3 oz.)

3 cloves garlic, finely chopped

1 tablespoon Italian seasoning

½ teaspoon salt

½ teaspoon pepper

1 can (28 oz.) crushed tomatoes, undrained

3½ cups uncooked penne pasta (about 12 ounces)

Shredded Parmesan cheese, if desired

Chopped fresh Italian (flat-leaf) parsley, if desired

Method

1. Spray 3 1/2-to 4-quart slow cookers with cooking spray. Place chicken in slow cooker and top with remaining ingredients except pasta, cheese, and parsley.
2. Cover; cook on low heat setting 6 to 8 hours. About 30 minutes before chicken is done, cook and drain pasta as directed on package.
3. Serve chicken with pasta. Garnish with cheese and parsley.

If you enjoy spicy food, add 1/4 teaspoon crushed red pepper flakes with the other seasonings.

Chicken thighs are a great choice for slow cooking, as the dark meat stays moist and flavorful. Boneless skinless thighs are now readily available at most grocery stores. If you prefer, you can substitute 2 lb boneless skinless chicken breasts.

Try whole grain penne or another whole grain pasta shape for added nutrition. Or instead of pasta, serve this chicken with garlic, mashed potatoes.

Slow Cooker Tuscan Pot Roast

· ·

Ingredients

1 package (1 oz.) dried mushrooms

1 cup hot water

2 cloves garlic, finely chopped

1 tablespoon grated lemon peel

1 teaspoon dried oregano leaves

½ teaspoon salt

1 boneless beef rump roast (2 1/2 pounds), trimmed of fat

1 can (14.5 oz.) diced tomatoes, undrained

1 cup frozen small whole onions (from 1 pound bag), thawed

½ cup dry red wine or beef flavored broth (from 32 oz. carton)

Method

In small bowl, place mushrooms and hot water; let stand 10 minutes.

Meanwhile, spray 4 to 5 quart slow cooker with cooking spray.

In small bowl, mix garlic, lemon peel, oregano and salt. Rub mixture over beef; place in cooker.

Drain mushrooms; coarsely chop. Top beef with the mushrooms, tomatoes, thawed onions, and wine.

Cover; cook on low heat setting 8 to 9 hours.

Remove beef from cooker; place on cutting board. Cover; let stand 10 minutes.

Cut beef into 8 serving pieces; serve with tomato mixture.

Serve with garlic mashed potatoes and slices of wheat bread.

Turkey Pot Roast with Sweet Potatoes and Cranberries

Ingredients

1 (2 to 3 pounds) boneless turkey breast

3 medium sweet potatoes, peeled, cubed (5 cups)

½ cup sweetened dried cranberries

6 green onions, cut into ½ inch pieces

¾ cup orange juice

½ teaspoon dried marjoram leaves

¼ teaspoon salt

2 tablespoons butter, melted

Method

1. Heat oven to 350°F. Place turkey breast in ungreased 13x9-inch (3-quart) baking dish.

2. Arrange sweet potatoes, cranberries and onions around turkey. Pour orange juice over top. Sprinkle with marjoram and salt. Cover with foil.

3. Bake at 350° degrees for 1 hour. Uncover; brush with melted butter. Bake an additional 30 minutes or until turkey is fork tender and juices run clear, spooning pan juices over turkey and vegetables once during baking. Serve turkey and vegetables with pan juices.

West Indian Chicken Roti

. . . .

Ingredients

Roti Shell

2½ cups all-purpose flour

2 teaspoons baking powder

1 tablespoon butter

¾ cup water

½ cup oil

Chicken Curry Stuffing

3 pounds chicken

2 tablespoons vegetable oil

1 large onion, chopped

3 clove garlic, minced

2 tablespoons curry powder

1 tablespoon chili powder

1 teaspoon paprika

2 cups water

Salt and pepper to taste

Method

1. Roti Shell: Sift 2 cups of flour, add baking powder and butter, and mix well. Add water, knead, and make a soft elastic but not sticky dough. Cut into six pieces. Roll each piece of dough thinly on floured board; apply oil to dough surface, sprinkle lightly with a pinch of flour. Fold in half, then quarter, roll up into a ball. Let stand for 15 minutes.

2. Roll out each piece thinly again, place on a hot griddle, and brush each side of dough with oil to prevent sticking, turn frequently. Remove Roti and clap with both hands, until

able to bend without breaking. Fold and place on waxed paper. Serve hot stuffed with chicken curry.

3. Chicken curry stuffing: Cut chicken into bite size pieces. In hot oil, sauté onions and garlic until tender, add curry powder. Add chicken pieces, salt pepper, chili powder and paprika. Cook on medium heat for 15 minutes. Add water, bring to a boil, then simmer, covered for about 25 minutes or until chicken is tender. Serve wrapped in a warm Roti.

Whiskey Braised Tenderloin

Ingredients

4 – 4 oz. beef tenderloin filets

1 oz. olive oil

3 oz. whiskey

Salt

Pepper

Method

1. Add salt and pepper to the tenderloin filets.
2. Add olive oil to a hot sauté pan, and add the tenderloin. Let the filets cook for approximately 2 minutes per side. To cook to medium, it will take about 6-7 minutes.
3. The meat is a little thicker, so you may have to adjust your heat so it cooks thoroughly.
4. Look for a nice carmelization or browning.
5. Once it has begun to brown, add the whiskey.

Pies, Tarts, Sandwiches and Foldovers

Almond Dutch Apple Tart

. . . .

Ingredients

Pastry:

1-1/2 cup all-purpose flour

3 tablespoons granulated sugar

¼ teaspoon salt

½ cup butter or margarine

1 egg

Filling:

5 tablespoons butter softened

2 eggs

1 teaspoon rum extract or brandy extract

1 can Almond Filling

1 can Dutch Apple Filling

To decorate: ¾ heavy cream, 1 tablespoon confectioners' sugar, ¼ cup toasted sliced almonds.

Method

Stir flour, granulated sugar, and salt in a medium size bowl until blended.
Cut in butter until mixture resembles coarse crumbs. Add eggs so dough blends together.
Press into bottom of a 9" or 10" fluted tart pan with removable bottom. Trim pastry even with rim of pan. Refrigerate for 30 minutes. Preheat 350°F

To make filling, beat butter in medium size bowl until fluffy. Add eggs and rum extract and beat with electric mixture until blended. Spread Dutch apple filling in bottom of pastry lined pan. Pour almond mixture evenly over filling.
Bake 40 to 45 minutes or until center is set and pastry is golden brown. Cool completely in pan on wire rack.

<u>To decorate</u>, use method above.

Whip cream in medium bowl with electric mixture until soft peaks form. Add confectioners sugar and whip until firm. Spoon whipped cream into pastry bag with a tip. Put on top of tart in decorate swirls. Sprinkle with toasted almonds and refrigerate until ready to serve. 10 to 12 servings.

Baked Egg and Toast Cups

Ingredients

6 slices wheat or white bread, crust removed

¼ cup melted butter

6 large eggs

¼ teaspoon salt

1/8 teaspoon ground black pepper

1/3 cup finely chopped grape tomatoes

¼ cup finely chopped red onion, optional

½ cup shredded sharp cheddar cheese

1 tablespoon fresh parsley, optional

TIP: If you prefer, you can scramble the eggs, then pour them into the toast cups

Method

1. Preheat oven to 350°F.
2. Coat 6 jumbo muffin cups with cooking spray. Brush both sides of trimmed bread slices with melted butter.
3. Press 1 bread slice into each muffin cup, molding it to the shape of the cup. The bread corners will rise out of the edges of the cup. Bake until lightly toasted, about 15 minutes.
4. Break 1 egg into each toast lined cup and season with salt and pepper. Add chopped tomatoes and onion, if using, dividing equally among muffin cups. Top with cheese and bake until cheese melts and eggs are set, 15 to 20 minutes. Scatter on parsley, if using.

Chicken and Roasted Pepper Sandwich

Ingredients

¼ cup olive oil

4 teaspoons red wine vinegar

1 tablespoon snipped fresh thyme

½ teaspoon salt

¼ teaspoon crushed red pepper

4 skinless, boneless chicken breast halves

4 1-inch bias cut slices Italian bread

¼ cup semi-soft cheese with herbs or semi-soft goat cheese

1 cup roasted red sweet peppers (about one 7 ounce jar), cut into strips

½ cup fresh basil, watercress, or baby spinach leaves

Method

1. Prepare a marinade in a small bowl whisking together oil, vinegar, thyme, salt, and crushed red pepper. Reserve 2 tablespoons of mixture; set aside.

2. Place each chicken breast between two sheets of plastic wrap; pound lightly with the flat side of a meat mallet to about ½ inch thickness. Place in a resealable plastic bag set in a shallow dish. Add remaining marinade; reseal bag. Marinate at room temperature about 15 minutes or in the refrigerator for up to 1 hour.

3. Grease the rack of an indoor electric grill. Preheat grill. Drain chicken, discarding marinade. Place chicken on the grill rack. Grill until chicken is no longer pink. For a covered grill, allow 3 to 4 minutes. Turn once halfway through grilling.

4. Brush cut sides of bread with reserved marinade. Place bread; cut sides down, on grill rack. Grill until lightly toasted. Turn once halfway through grilling then remove bread from grill.

5. To serve, place a chicken breast on each grilled bread slice. Spread with cheese. Top each sandwich with sweet pepper and basil.

Makes 4 sandwiches.

Chicken Salad Sandwich

Ingredients

1 rotisserie chicken, about 2 ¼ pounds

¾ cup mayonnaise

¾ cup finely chopped celery

2 tablespoons dill pickle relish

1 tablespoon chopped fresh tarragon

½ teaspoon salt

¼ teaspoon ground black pepper

12 thin slices of bread

6 leaves romaine lettuce, torn

Method

1. Using your fingers, remove and discard the skin, bones, and excess fat from the chicken, placing the chicken meat in a large bowl. Tear or chop meat (you should have about 3 1/2 cups).

2. Add mayonnaise, celery, relish, tarragon, salt, and pepper to the bowl. Stir until thoroughly combined. Spoon onto the bread, adding a lettuce leaf to each sandwich.

TIP: If you don't have a country loaf, try sourdough rolls or thinly sliced white whole grain, honey wheat or rye loaf.

Delicious Tuna Fish Salad Sandwiches

. . . .

Ingredients

1 large can 12 ounces solid white tuna fish packed in water, drained and flaked

2 stalks celery, finely chopped

1 small onion, finely chopped

3 tablespoons low calorie mayonnaise

½ teaspoon black pepper

1 teaspoon hot sauce

1 teaspoon fresh lemon juice

1 teaspoon dill weed

1 medium tomato, sliced

Several lettuce leaves

2-4 slices of whole wheat bread

Method

1. Open tuna remove from can, drain water, flake and set aside

2. Chop the following ingredients; celery, onion and set aside.

3. In a large bowl, mix drained tuna, 3 tablespoons of mayonnaise thoroughly, and add chopped onion and celery, black pepper, hot sauce, lemon juice and dill weed. Stir ingredients until everything is mixed into tuna.

4. Spoon mixture onto slice of whole wheat bread, add lettuce and tomato covering bread evenly, and finish with another slice of whole wheat on top. Serve with grapes or an apple and enjoy.

Easy Apple Pie Foldover

Ingredients

*When you don't want to bake a big
pie, make a four serving foldover
that's every bit as scrumptious!*

1 1/2 cups thinly sliced, peeled apples (1
1/2 medium)

1/4 cup packed brown sugar

2 tablespoons water

1 teaspoon lemon juice

1 tablespoon all-purpose flour

1 tablespoon granulated sugar

¼ teaspoon salt

1 tablespoon butter or margarine

½ teaspoon vanilla

1 box refrigerated pie crusts

1 egg

Method

In 2 quart saucepan, mix apples, brown sugar, 1 tablespoon of the water and the lemon juice. Cook over medium heat, stirring occasionally, until bubbly. Reduce heat to low; cover and cook 6 to 8 minutes, stirring occasionally, until apples are tender.

In small bowl, mix flour, granulated sugar and salt. Gradually stir into apple mixture, cooking and stirring until mixture thickens. Remove from heat; stir in butter and vanilla. Cool 15 minutes.

Meanwhile, heat oven to 375°F. Let pie crust pouch stand at room temperature for 15 minutes.

Remove pie crust from pouch; unroll crust on ungreased cookie sheet. Spoon cooled fruit mixture evenly onto half of crust to within 1/2 inch of edge.

In small bowl, beat egg and 1 tablespoon water; brush over edge of crust. Fold untopped half of crust over apple mixture; firmly press edge to seal. Flute edge; cut small slits in several places in top crust. Brush top with remaining egg mixture.

Bake 25 to 35 minutes or until crust is golden brown. Serve warm or cool. Makes 4 servings

Easy Cherry Tarts

Ingredients

1 tube (8 oz.) refrigerated crescent rolls

1 package (3 oz.) cream cheese, softened

¼ cup confectioners' sugar

1 cup canned cherry pie filling

¼ teaspoon almond extract

Method

1. Place crescent dough in a lightly floured surface; seal seams and perforations. Cut into 24 pieces; press onto the bottoms and up the sides of greased miniature muffin cups.

2. In a small bowl, beat cream cheese and confectioners' sugar until smooth. Place about ½ teaspoon in each cup. Combine pie filling and extract, place about 2 teaspoons in each cup.

3. Bake at 375 degrees for 12-14 minutes or until edges are lightly browned. Remove to wire racks to cool. Refrigerate until serving. Yield 2 dozen.

Florentine Crepe Cups

Ingredients

2/3 cup all-purpose flour
½ teaspoon salt
3 eggs
1 cup milk

Filling:
1½ cups (6 oz.) shredded cheddar cheese
3 tablespoons all-purpose flour
1 package (10 oz.) frozen chopped spinach, thawed and squeezed dry
1 can (4 oz.) mushroom stems and pieces, drained 2/3 cup mayonnaise
3 eggs, lightly beaten, 6 bacon strips, cooked and crumbled
½ teaspoon salt and pepper to taste

Method

1. In a bowl, whisk the flour, salt, eggs and milk until smooth.
2. Heat a lightly greased 8 inch nonstick skillet; add 3 tablespoons of batter. Lift and tilt pan to evenly coat bottom. Cook for 2 minutes or until top appears dry.
3. Place in a greased muffin cup. Repeat with the remaining batter.
4. In a bowl, combine the filling ingredients.
5. Place ¼ cup of filling in each crepe cup. Bake, uncovered, at 350 degrees for 30 minutes or until eggs are completely set. Makes 6 servings.

Mini Ice Cream Cookie Cups

• •

Make-ahead recipe Is an impressive dessert for your next gathering

Ingredients

1 package 16 oz. refrigerated sugar cookies

4 teaspoons sugar

1/3 cup finely chopped walnuts

½ cup semi-sweet chocolate baking chips

¼ cup seedless red raspberry jam

1 ½ cups vanilla bean ice cream, softened

24 fresh raspberries

Method

1. Heat oven to 350 degrees. Spray 24 mini muffin cups with nonstick cooking spray. Place 1 cookie dough round in each muffin cup. Bake 15 to 20 minutes or until golden brown.

2. Place 2 teaspoons of the sugar in small bowl. Dip end of a wooden spoon handle in sugar; carefully press into center of each cookie to make 1-inch wide indentation. Cool completely in pan, for about 15 minutes.

3. Meanwhile, in a small bowl, mix walnuts and remaining 2 teaspoons sugar; set aside. In a small microwavable bowl, microwave chocolate chips uncovered on high 30 to 60 seconds, stirring after 30 seconds, until smooth.

4. Run knife around edges of cups to loosen, gently remove from pan. Dip rim of each cup into melted chocolate, then into walnut mixture. Place walnut side up on cookie sheet with sides.

5. In another small microwavable bowl, microwave jam uncovered on high about 15 seconds until melted. Spoon ½ teaspoon jam into each cup. Freeze cups about 5 minutes or until chocolate is set.

6. Spoon ice cream into cups, using small cookie scoop or measuring tablespoon. Top each cup with fresh raspberry; serve immediately. Makes 24 tartlets

To Make Ahead: Prepare cookie cups through step 5 omitting jam. Store covered up to two days at room temperature. When ready to serve fill with jam, ice cream and top with raspberry.

Pumpkin Pie

Ingredients

2 eggs, beaten
¾ cup brown sugar
½ teaspoon salt
¼ teaspoon cloves
1 teaspoon vanilla
1 can evaporated milk

2 cups pumpkin
½ teaspoon ginger
¼ cup dark rum
1 teaspoon cinnamon
1 teaspoon fresh ground nutmeg
1 (10 inch) pie crust (not baked)

Method

1. Mix all ingredients with a whisk. Add to unbaked pie shell. Bake for 15 minutes at 425° degrees, then lower oven to 350° degrees for 35 minutes until knife inserted comes out clean. Cool.

Whipped Topping
2 cups heavy whipping cream, beaten
¼ cup powdered sugar
1 tablespoon dark rum

Beat whipped topping ingredients together and serve on pie.

Quesadillas

Quesadillas are a good way to "hide" meat and vegetables.

Ingredients

Whole Wheat Tortillas
Refried Black Beans
Meat (chicken, turkey, fish, lean beef)
Monterrey Jack and Cheddar Cheese
Sliced Avocado
Sliced Tomato.

Method

1. Top a whole wheat tortilla with: refried black beans, meat (chicken, turkey, fish, lean beef).
2. Monterrey jack and cheddar cheese, sliced avocado, sliced tomato.
3. Place a second whole-wheat tortilla on top and cook in a skillet.

Streusel Topped Pumpkin Pie

Ingredients

1 box refrigerated pie crusts, softened as directed on box

Filling

1 can (15 oz.) pumpkin (not pumpkin pie mix)
1 can (12 oz.) evaporated milk (1-1/2 cups)
½ cup granulated sugar
2 eggs, slightly beaten
1½ teaspoons pumpkin pie spice
¼ teaspoon salt

Streusel

¼ cup packed brown sugar
2 tablespoons all-purpose flour
2 tablespoons butter or margarine, softened
½ cup chopped pecans

Topping

1 teaspoon grated orange peel

1 container (8 oz.) frozen whipped topping, thawed (3 cups)

Method

1. Heat oven to 425°F. Place pie crust in 9 inch glass pie pan as directed on box for One-Crust Filled Pie.
2. In large bowl, mix filling ingredients until well blended. Pour into crust-lined pan.
3. Bake 15 minutes. Reduce oven temperature to 350°F; bake 15 minutes. Meanwhile, in small bowl, mix streusel ingredients.
4. Sprinkle streusel over pumpkin filling. Bake 15 to 20 minutes longer or until knife inserted in center comes out clean. Cool completely, about 1 hour.
5. Gently fold orange peel into whipped topping. Serve pie with topping. Store in refrigerator. Yield 8 servings.

Sweet Potato Pie

Ingredients

1 pound sweet potatoes

½ cup butter, softened

1/4 cup white sugar

½ cup milk

2 eggs

½ teaspoon ground nutmeg

½ teaspoon ground cinnamon

1 teaspoon vanilla extract

1 deep dish 9 inch unbaked pie crust

Method

1. Peel sweet potato and cut in 2 inch pieces. Put pieces in a small pan of water to cook until soft for about 20 minutes. Drain water when cooked.

2. In a bowl break sweet potato pieces apart. Add butter, and mix well and add sugar, milk, eggs, nutmeg, cinnamon and vanilla. Beat well until smooth. Pour filling into an unbaked piecrust.

3. Bake at 350 degrees F for 40 to 45 minutes until golden brown or until knife inserted in center comes out clean. Pie may drop down as it cools.

NOTE: If white sweet potato is used, ¼ cup sugar may be used. The yellow sweet potato can use ½ cup sugar. The white sweet potato is sweeter.

Tiny Raspberry Cheesecake Tarts

Ingredients

2 oz. bittersweet or semisweet chocolate, cut up

½ teaspoon shortening

1 2.1 oz. package baked miniature Phyllo dough shells

3 oz. package cream cheese, softened

2 tablespoons dairy sour cream

2 tablespoons powdered sugar

2 teaspoons raspberry liqueur or milk

15 fresh raspberries

Method

1. In a small saucepan, stir the cut up chocolate and shortening over low heat until melted.
2. Remove pan from heat. Brush the inside (bottom and sides) of each phyllo shell evenly with the melted chocolate mixture.
3. Return each shell to plastic tray included in package. Chill phyllo shells in refrigerator about 20 minutes or until chocolate is set.
4. In a small bowl, stir together the cream cheese, sour cream, and powdered sugar until smooth.
5. Stir in liqueur or milk. Transfer mixture to a small resealable plastic bag; seal bag.
6. Snip off a corner of the bag. Pipe about 1 teaspoon of the cream cheese mixture into each shell. Cover tarts loosely; chill 2 to 4 hours.
7. If desired, garnish each tart with a fresh raspberry and mint leaves. Makes 15 tarts.

Tuna Turnovers

Ingredients

2 hard-cooked eggs

1 can 6½ ounces water packed tuna, drained

¼ cup chopped celery finely chopped

¼ cup thinly sliced green onion

½ cup mayonnaise

Salt and pepper to taste

1 package 10 ounces refrigerated buttermilk biscuits

1 cup shredded Cheddar cheese

1 egg beaten

Method

Bake at 350°F for 20 minutes.

1. Position wire rack in lower guides of oven and set at 350°F.
2. Meanwhile, line baking dish with aluminum foil.
3. Mash eggs coarsely in mixing bowl. Add tuna, celery, onion, mayonnaise, salt, and pepper and blend well. Unroll dough and separate into 4 rectangles, smoothing perforated lines together.
4. Sprinkle ¼ cup cheese over half of each rectangle.
5. Divide tuna mixture evenly over cheese. Fold dough over tuna mixture, to seal edges.
6. Transfer to dish. Brush turnovers with beaten egg.
7. Place dish in oven to bake.

Makes 4 servings

Turkey Apple and Swiss Melt Sandwich

. . . .

Ingredients

1 tablespoon mustard

1 teaspoon honey

8 slices whole wheat bread

4 1-oz. slices Swiss cheese

5 oz. thinly slices granny smith apple (about 1 small apple)

8 oz. thinly sliced lower sodium deli turkey

Cooking Spray

Method

1. Combine mustard and honey in a small bowl.

2. Spread on one side of each of 4 slices with 1 ½ teaspoon of mustard mixture.

3. Place one cheese slice on dressed side of bread slices and each with 5 slices and 2 ounces turkey. Top sandwich with remaining 4 bread slices. Coat both sides of sandwiches with cooking spray.

4. Heat a large nonstick skillet over medium high heat. Add sandwiches to pan. Cook 2 minutes on each side or until bread is browned and cheese melts.

Zucchini Apple Pie

Ingredients

4 cups zucchini

2 tablespoons lemon juice

Dash of salt

1 ½ cup sugar

1 ¼ teaspoon cream of tartar

3 tablespoons flour

1 ½ teaspoon cinnamon

½ teaspoon nutmeg

2 teaspoons vanilla

2 tablespoons butter

2 ready made pie crusts

Method

Peel zucchini, cut lengthwise into quarters. Remove the seeds and slice crosswise. They will look just like apple slices.

Cook for 3 to 4 minutes in a 6 quart saucepan in 1 cup of water on top of the stove until tender. Drain all the water off and leave the zucchini in the pot.

Add lemon, salt, sugar, cream of tartar, flour, cinnamon, nutmeg and vanilla. Stir well. It will be runny, but that is okay.

Prepare the crust in a 9 inch pie pan according to Ready Made Crust directions. Put the zucchini mixture into the pie crust and dot with butter. Add the top crust and make small slits in it. Sprinkle a teaspoon of sugar over the top.

Bake at 400 degrees for 40 minutes. Let it cool completely before serving. Refrigerate any leftover pie.

Erdbeerbowle
mit Rotwein

Melonenbowle

Erdbeerbowle
mit Weißwein

Punch

Banana Punch

. . . .

Ingredients

4 ripe bananas

¾ pint water

¼ pint evaporated milk

¼ teaspoon freshly grated nutmeg

3-4 drops of vanilla essence

Honey to sweeten

Method

Peel the bananas. Mash them with a fork and pass the puree through a fine sieve or liquidize with an electric blender. Add the water, evaporated milk, vanilla and nutmeg. Sweeten to taste with honey. Chill before serving.

Serves 3-4

Caribbean Cream Stout Punch

. . . .

This fairly unusual punch, made using stout, evaporated milk and sherry, is a well-known "Pick-Me-Up that is popular all over the Caribbean. With a sweet, heady aroma of vanilla, it soothes and revives tired minds and bodies.

Ingredients

16 fluid oz. bottle stout (2 cups)
1 1/4 cup evaporated milk
5 tablespoons condensed milk
5 teaspoons sherry
2 or 3 drops vanilla essence
Freshly grated nutmeg

Method

1. Mix together the stout, evaporated and condensed milks, sherry and vanilla essence in a blender or food processor, or whisk together in a large mixing bowl, until creamy.

2. Add a little grated nutmeg to the stout mixture and blend or whisk thoroughly again for a few minutes.

3. Chill for at least 45 minutes, or until really cold, before ladling into small glasses to serve.

Makes 2 servings.

Caribbean Mango Punch

· ·

Ingredients

¼ cup water

¼ cup sugar

3 cups mango juice

2 cups orange juice

1 cup pineapple juice

1 tablespoon limejuice

Method

In a small saucepan, bring the water and sugar to a boil. Boil for 10 minutes, stirring constantly. Let the syrup cool. In a large bowl, stir together the sugar syrup, mango juice, orange juice, pineapple juice and lime juice. Chill.

Serve over crushed ice.

1 to 2 servings

Cashew Nut Milk

Ingredients

3½ cups blanched cashews

1 cup caster (superfine) sugar

¼ teaspoon ground cinnamon

3½ cups boiling water

Method

1. Finely grind the cashews in a food processor. Add the sugar and cinnamon and grind the mixture again to make a smooth paste.

2. With the motor still running, gradually pour in 3 ¾ cups of boiling water, until the drink becomes smooth and frothy. Scrape down the mixture occasionally, if necessary.

3. Pour the cashew nut milk into a pitcher. Cover and chill in the refrigerator. Stir well before serving in tall glasses. Add ice cubes in each glass. As the ice melts, it will dilute the drink, giving it a lighter texture.

This Cuban version with cashews is even more delicious. The result is rich and creamy. It is great for kids and even better for adults that may need a hangover cure. In Madrid, Spain and Mexico they have a similar drink that is made with almonds.

Homemade Ginger Ale

Ingredients

2 cups fresh ginger cut into 1/8 inch slices
(about 2 large handfuls)
2 cups sugar
4 cups water
1 quart club soda, well chilled
1 lime, quartered

Method

1. Make ginger syrup. Combine the ginger, 2 cups of the sugar, and the water in a medium saucepan and bring to a boil over high heat.

2. Reduce the heat and simmer until syrupy or reduced by half, for 40 to 50 minutes. The syrup will thicken as it cools so don't over reduce it. Strain the syrup and reserve the ginger.

3. To make ginger ale, fill four 8 ounces glasses with club soda. Pour two tablespoons of the ginger syrup down the side of each glass. Garnish with a lime wedge on the rim of each glass.

Makes 4 servings.

Kool Aid Punch

Ingredients

- 1 packet raspberry Kool Aid
- 1 packet strawberry Kool Aid
- 2 cups sugar (or less)
- 4 quarts water
- 2 small cans frozen orange juice
- 2 small cans frozen lemonade

Method

Mix all ingredients together and serve as is or add 7-up

Mango Papaya Punch

Ingredients

1 small papaya

1 19-oz. can mango nectar

1 cup sugar

3 cups water

Juice of 2 limes

1 liter club soda or quart

3 ounces light rum (optional)

Method

1. Peel the papaya and remove its seeds.
2. Combine the papaya, mango nectar, sugar, water, and limejuice in blender.
3. Process for approximately 30 seconds, or until well blended.
4. Chill for at least 1 hour.
5. Mix in the club soda and rum just before serving. Serve in your most attractive punch cups.
6. If possible, decorate the punch bowl with hibiscus blossoms.

8 to 10 servings

Orange Julius

Ingredients

6 oz. frozen orange juice concentrate

1 cup milk

1 cup water

½ cup sugar

1 teaspoon vanilla extract

8-9 ice cubes

Method

1. Combine all ingredients except ice cubes in blender.
2. Blend for about 1-2 minutes, adding ice cubes one at a time.

Peanut Butter Milkshakes

. . . .

Ingredients

1 cup milk

2 cups vanilla ice cream

½ cup peanut butter

2 teaspoon sugar

Method

1. Combine all ingredients. Cover and process in blender for 30 seconds.
2. Pour into chilled glasses; serve immediately. 3 Servings.

Peanut Punch

Ingredients

8 oz. shelled roasted peanuts

1½ pint water

½ pint evaporated milk or Soya milk

½ teaspoon vanilla essence

½ teaspoon freshly grated nutmeg

Raw cane sugar

Method

Place the shelled peanuts in an electric blender or food processor. Measure out 1 pint of the water and gradually pour this into the blender while grinding the peanuts. Leave the blender running for 1-2 minutes until the peanuts are thoroughly blended. Strain the mixture through a sieve, pouring in a little at a time and squeeze to extract all the liquid. After squeezing, discard the contents. Repeat until all the peanut mixture is used up. Add milk, and sweeten the drink to taste with cane sugar and flavor with vanilla essence and grated nutmeg.

Pineapple Citrus Punch

Ingredients

3 cups pineapple juice, chilled

3 cups orange grapefruit juice, chilled

1 quart lemon lime carbonated beverage chilled

1 cup lime or lemon sherbet

Method

Mix juices and carbonated beverage in large punch bowl.

Spoon one scoop of sherbet into bowl. Serve immediately

Makes 19 servings about ½ cup each

Ingredients

1 bottle 25.6 oz. pink sparkling grape juice

1 (10 oz.) package frozen Raspberries

Method

Chill one bottle 25.6 oz. pink sparkling grape juice.

Cut one package (10 oz.) frozen raspberries into fourths.

Place raspberries and one cup grape juice in a blender.

Cover and blend on high speed for 15 seconds.

Strain and pour remaining grape juice into small punch bowl or pitcher.

Stir in raspberry mixture. Serve immediately.

8 Servings (about ½ cup each)

Rum Punch

. . . .

This punch came from a rum distillery in Guyana, where some of the finest rum in the world is made, and the tantalizing aromas of sugar cane and rum pervade the air.

Ingredients

2/3 cup orange juice

2/3 cup pineapple juice

2/3 cup mango juice

½ cup water

½ cup dark rum

One shake of angostura bitters

Freshly grated nutmeg

2 teaspoon raw sugar

1 small banana

1 large orange

Method

1. Pour the orange, pineapple and mango juices into a large punch bowl. Stir in water.

2. Add the rum, angostura bitters, nutmeg and sugar. Stir gently for a few minutes until the sugar has dissolved.

3. Slice the banana thinly and stir the slices gently into the punch.

4. Slice the orange and add to the punch. Chill and serve in tumblers with ice.

Variations: You can use white rum instead of dark, if you prefer. To make a stronger punch, simply add more rum.

Salads

Avocado Salad

· ·

Ingredients

1 large ripe avocado

2 teaspoon limejuice

1 medium sized onion

3 medium sized tomatoes

¼ cabbage or whole Chinese leaf

Method

Cut the avocado lengthways into thick slices. Remove the skin and stone and cut avocado into thick slices. Discard stone and sprinkle the limejuice over the slices. Peel the onion and slice into fine rings. Slice the tomatoes. Wash the cabbage or Chinese leaf, drain and shred finely. Arrange a bed of shredded cabbage on a serving plate, top with the avocado slices and garnish with tomato and onion. Serve immediately.

Serve 4

Bean and Pepper Salad

Ingredients

4 oz. red kidney beans

4 oz. black eyed beans

1 red pepper

1 green pepper

1 yellow pepper

4 tablespoons peanut oil

1 teaspoon vinegar

Juice of 1 lime

Freshly ground black pepper

Method

Soak the kidney beans and black eye beans separately in plenty of cold water overnight. In separate saucepans cover the beans with fresh water, bring to a boil and simmer for 1 hour until they are soft. Drain and cool. Cut off the stem end of the peppers and scoop out the seeds; slice the peppers into thin rings. Mix the dressing ingredients, the oil, the vinegar, limejuice and black pepper, beating with a fork. Combine the beans in a serving dish and pour over the dressing. Arrange the peppers on top of the beans.

Serves 4

This is a beautifully colored salad. The red and white of the beans topped with the symbolic red, yellow and green of the peppers. Preparations need to begin a day in advance to allow time for soaking the beans.

Berry Best Salad

Ingredients

¼ cup orange juice

1 tablespoon salad oil

2 teaspoons honey mustard or Dijon-style mustard

1 teaspoon sugar

¼ teaspoon salt

4 cups lettuce

1-1/2 cups fresh blueberries, raspberries, quartered strawberries,

and/or canned mandarin orange sections, drained.

2 tablespoons bite-size cheddar fish-shaped or

Pretzel crackers or 1 tablespoon shelled sunflower seeds.

Method

1. For dressing, in a screw top jar combine orange juice, oil, mustard, sugar, and salt.

2. Cover and shake until combined. Place lettuce in medium bowl. Drizzle with dressing; toss to coat. Divide lettuce among 4 plates.

3. Arrange fruit on lettuce. Sprinkle with crackers. Serve immediately.

Broccoli Salad

Ingredients

- 1 bunch of broccoli, separated into florets
- 1 head cauliflower, separated into florets
- 8 strips bacon, cooked and crumbled
- 1 cup chopped tomato, seeded
- 1/3 cup chopped onion
- 1 cup mayonnaise or salad dressing
- 1/3 cup sugar
- 2 tablespoon vinegar

NOTE: You can substitute miracle whip light for the mayonnaise and also for the sugar, you can use Splenda.

Method

In a large salad bowl, combine broccoli, cauliflower, bacon, tomatoes, and onion. Set aside. In another bowl, combine mayonnaise, sugar, and vinegar. Mix until smooth. Just before serving, pour dressing over salad and toss.

Carrot Slaw With Apples

Ingredients

2 tablespoons orange juice

1 tablespoon lemon juice

1 tablespoon honey

1 tablespoon reduced fat sour cream

1/4 teaspoon pumpkin pie spice

1/4 teaspoon salt

Pinch of ground black pepper

2 cups matchstick cut carrots

1 cup matchstick cut apples

1 cup dried cherries

Method

1. In a medium bowl, whisk together orange juice, lemon juice, honey, sour cream, pumpkin-pie spice, salt, and pepper.
2. Add carrots, apples, and cherries, and toss to mix.

TIP: To switch up the flavor, replace the pumpkin-pie spice with cinnamon or apple pie spice. Or for something more exotic, use 1/2 teaspoon curry powder.

Chicken Rice Waldorf Salad

Ingredients

- 1 ½ cup instant brown rice
- 1 cup reduced calorie dressing
- 1 large red apple diced
- 1 tablespoon lemon juice
- 2 cups cooked chicken
- 1 cup diced celery
- 1 cup seedless green grapes

Method

Prepare rice as directed. Mix in reduced calorie dressing. Mix in apple and lemon juice and stir into rice mixture with remaining ingredients.

Ingredients

- 1 1/3 cup sour cream
- 1 1/3 cup mayonnaise
- 2 teaspoon minced onion
- 2 teaspoons parsley
- 2 teaspoons dill weed

Method

Mix all ingredients together. Serve with carrots, celery, and cucumber and your choice of other vegetables.

Green Bananas and Salt Fish Salad

Ingredients

Two medium sized green bananas

Three teaspoons of mayonnaise

¼ pound salt fish

½ cup mixed vegetables

Two cloves garlic minced

¼ cup chopped celery and parsley

One lime juice

Method

Squeeze a lime in a pot of water. This will prevent the green bananas from getting black after you peel them. Skin your green bananas and place them into the pot of water as soon as you finish peeling each green banana.

Clean each banana by removing any extra skin that may have been left on it and place them in the pot that you are going to use to boil them in.

Remove the scales that are on the salt fish and wash off the excess salt that is on it (preferably running water). Put the green bananas in the pot and allow it to cook. This normally takes about 30 minutes to cook.

Do not add any salt to the pot with the green bananas or salt fish.

Insert a fork in the bananas to test if it is cooked. If they are soft then you can turn it off and drain out the excess water. Put the mixed vegetables in a container and pour out some of the boiled water onto it.

Mash the bananas with a fork. Add the chopped celery, parsley and garlic. Shred the salt fish when you're adding it to the bowl with all the ingredients. Mix them together and allow it to cool down.

When it is cooled down, throw out the water and add the mixed vegetables along with the mayonnaise and mix them together. This great recipe can be prepared in St Lucia, West Indies, anywhere in the world where you can get green bananas.

Grilled Greek Chicken Salad

. . . .

Ingredients

1 ¼ pound uncooked chicken breast tenders (not breaded)

2 teaspoons olive or vegetable oil

2 teaspoons Greek seasoning

1 bag (10 oz.) washed fresh baby spinach leaves

1 medium cucumber, peeled, seeded and diced

1 cup halved grape or cherry tomatoes

¼ cup halved pitted olives

2/3 cup vinaigrette dressing

¼ cup crumbled feta cheese

Method

1. Heat gas or charcoal grill. Toss chicken tenders with oil; sprinkle with Greek seasoning.

2. Place chicken on grill over medium heat. Cover grill; cook 5 to 6 minutes, turning once, until no longer pink in center.

3. Meanwhile, in large bowl, toss spinach, cucumber, tomatoes and olives with dressing. Spoon onto 4 serving plates; serve with chicken tenders. Sprinkle with feta cheese.

4. If chicken tenders are not available, cut boneless skinless chicken breasts lengthwise into thin strips.

5. Almost any savory vinaigrette, or oil-and-vinegar dressing, would work with this recipe. Several brands of plain vinaigrettes are available, plus ones with balsamic vinegar and various herbs.

Serves 4

Lentil Salad

Ingredients

- 1 cup dry brown lentils
- 1 cup diced carrots
- 1 cup diced onion
- 2 teaspoons lemon juice
- ½ teaspoon thyme
- ¼ cup chopped parsley
- ¼ teaspoon ground black pepper
- ¼ cup olive oil
- 2 teaspoons minced garlic
- ½ cup diced celery
- 1 teaspoon salt

Method

1. Wash lentils and add two cups of water and boil in saucepan for 20 minutes or until tender.

2. Sauté onion in ¼ cup oil, add carrots, garlic, celery, parsley, and thyme in a large saucepan for 15 minutes till tender.

3. Add cooked lentil to mixture. Reduce heat; toss to mix. Add salt, pepper, and lemon juice and simmer uncovered for 10 to 15 minutes until lentils are tender. Serve at room temperature.

Mexican Garden Salad

Ingredients

1 pound ground chuck

1 jar 16 oz. thick and chunky salsa, divided

¼ cup water

1 envelope taco seasoning

1 ½ heads iceberg lettuce, torn

3 cups broccoli florets about ½ pound

1 small red onion, thinly sliced into rings

1 medium carrot, shredded

1 large tomato, chopped

1 can (4 oz.) chopped green chilies, drained

½ to 1 cup shredded cheddar cheese

1 cup 8 ounces sour cream

Tortilla chips, optional

Method

1. In a skillet, cook ground beef over medium heat until no longer pink, drain. Add 1 cup salsa, water and taco seasoning; bring to a boil. Reduce heat and simmer for 20 minutes; cool.

2. In a 3 or 4 quart glass bowl, layer vegetables in order given. Top with chilies, beef mixture and cheese. Combine sour cream and remaining salsa; serve with salad and tortilla chips if desired. Yield 6-8 servings.

Pineapple Pretzel Salad

. . . .

Ingredients

2 cups crushed pretzels

½ cup sugar

1 stick butter

1 (8 oz.) package cream cheese

½ cup sugar

1 (20 oz.) can pineapple with juice

1 (8 oz.) carton whipped topping

Method

Melt butter in 9 x 13 pan. Mix in sugar and pretzels. Bake at 400 degrees for 8 minutes. Stir; turn off oven and leave in until cool. Mix together the cream cheese, sugar and pineapple with juice. Fold in whipped topping. Before serving add pretzel mixture.

Sweet and Sour Broccoli Salad

Ingredients

1 bunch of broccoli, separated into florets

½ head cauliflower

1 red pepper

8 oz. fresh mushrooms

1 bunch scallions

Dressing

¾ cup wine vinegar

¼ cup olive oil

½ cup sugar or use 2-3 packets Splenda

1/8 teaspoon salt

1 teaspoon paprika

1 teaspoon onion powder

1 teaspoon celery seed

Method

Wash broccoli and cauliflower and break into bite size pieces. Cut red pepper into thin strips. Slice mushrooms and chop scallions. Place the vegetables into a large plastic container with a tight fitting lid. Combine dressing ingredients in a bowl or jar. Blend thoroughly and add dressing to vegetables 1 hour before serving. Toss or shake occasionally while chilling. Makes 8 servings

Warm Winter Salad

Ingredients

3 strips bacon

3 tablespoons olive oil

2 tablespoons red wine vinegar or balsamic vinegar

1 teaspoon dijon mustard (optional)

1 small garlic clove, minced

1/8 teaspoon salt

1/8 teaspoon ground black pepper

1 bunch (10 oz.) spinach, coarse stems trimmed (about 5 cups loosely packed)

1 McIntosh apple (4 oz.), peeled and cut into ½ inch pieces

8 shavings (3/4 oz.) Romano cheese, each about 1 inch by 2 inches

Method

Cook the bacon in a skillet over medium-low heat, turning the slices occasionally until crisp and browned, 8 to 10 minutes.

Drain on a paper towel-lined plate and keep warm. Measure the fat in the pan (there should be 2 to 3 tablespoons). Add enough oil to equal 5 tablespoons of total fat in the pan. Whisk the vinegar, mustard (if using), garlic, salt, and pepper into the fat in the pan. Keep warm.

In a large bowl, combine the spinach and apple. Spoon the warm dressing over the spinach and apple. Toss to coat. Divide among four warmed plates, crumble the bacon over the spinach, and top with the cheese.

Seafood

Baked Tilapia

Tilapia coated with light mayo and seasonings – a great way to enjoy fish.

Ingredients

- 1 teaspoon lemon pepper
- 1 sprig dill weed
- ¼ teaspoon or 1 packet spicy mustard
- 1 dash seasoned salt
- 1 tablespoon light mayonnaise
- 4 ounces tilapia fillets

NOTE: A baked potato and a lettuce salad may complete this meal.

Method

1. Rinse fish with cold water and sprinkle with a dash of seasoned salt.
2. Combine mayonnaise, lemon pepper, small squirt of spicy mustard, and sprinkle of dill weed.
3. Coat fish with dressing mixture.
4. Bake at 425°F for 8-10 minutes until fish flakes easily with a fork.

Caribbean Grill Basket Scallops

. . . .

Add something flavorful to your family's Caribbean cuisine dinner! Serve grilled scallops brushed with butter mixture and ready in 15 minutes.

Ingredients

2 tablespoons butter, melted

2 tablespoons fresh orange juice

1 teaspoon Caribbean or jerk seasoning

1 teaspoon grated orange peel

1/8 teaspoon crushed red pepper flakes

1 pound (13 to 16) fresh sea scallops, drained

Method

1. Heat the grill. In medium bowl, combine all ingredients except scallops; mix well.
2. Add scallops; toss to coat.
3. With slotted spoon, place scallops in grill basket; reserve butter mixture. Place basket on gas grill over medium heat or on charcoal grill 4 to 6 inches from medium coals. Cook 3 to 8 minutes or until scallops turn opaque, turning and brushing twice with butter mixture. Discard any remaining butter mixture.

Caribbean Seafood Stew

Ingredients

2 teaspoons olive oil

1 teaspoon lime juice

¼ teaspoon salt

1/8 teaspoon pepper

1 pound skinless orange roughy or red snapper fillets, cut into 1 inch cubes

1 cup chopped onion

1 cup chopped green sweet pepper

6 cloves garlic, minced (1 teaspoon)

1 jalapeno pepper, seeded and finely chopped

1 14-1/2 oz. can diced tomatoes

½ cup unsweetened coconut milk

8 oz. peeled and deveined uncooked medium shrimp

½ cup snipped cilantro

2 cups hot cooked rice

2 tablespoons snipped fresh cilantro

bottled hot pepper sauce (optional)

Method

1. In a medium bowl, stir together 1 tablespoon of the olive oil, lime juice, salt, and pepper. Add fish cubes; toss to coat. Set aside.

2. In a 3 quart saucepan, heat remaining oil over medium high heat. Add the onion, sweet pepper, garlic, and jalapeno. Cook and stir 4 minutes until onion is tender but not brown. Stir in undrained tomatoes and coconut milk. Bring to boiling; reduce heat. Simmer, uncovered for 10 minutes, stirring occasionally. Stir in shrimp, fish mixture, and ½ cup cilantro. Return to boiling and reduce heat. Simmer, uncovered for 5 minutes or until fish just flakes easily with a fork and shrimp turn opaque, stirring occasionally. Serve over hot rice. Sprinkle with remaining cilantro. Pass hot pepper sauce, if desired. Makes 4 to 6 servings.

Citrus Glazed Salmon

. . . .

Ingredients

1 2-pound fresh or frozen salmon fillet, skin removed

Salt and ground black pepper

¾ cup orange marmalade

2 green onions sliced (1/4 cup)

1 clove garlic minced

2 teaspoons dry white wine

1 teaspoon grated fresh ginger

1 teaspoon mustard

1 teaspoon cayenne pepper

1/8 teaspoon five-spice powder

3 tablespoons sliced almonds, toasted

Steamed asparagus (optional)

Method

1. Thaw fish, if frozen. Preheat oven to 450 degrees. Rinse fish; pat dry with paper towels. Season salmon with salt and pepper. Place in a shallow baking pan; set aside.

2. In a small bowl combine together marmalade, green onions, garlic, wine, ginger, mustard, cayenne pepper, and five-spice powder. Spoon mixture over salmon.

3. Bake, uncovered, for 4 to 6 minutes per ½ inch thickness or until salmon flakes easily when tested with a fork. Transfer fish and glaze to a serving dish. Sprinkle with almonds. Serve with steamed asparagus, if desired.

Makes 8 servings

Drunken Catfish

. . . .

Ingredients

¼ cup bourbon

1 cup soy sauce

¼ cup local honey

3 tablespoons sesame oil

2 teaspoons minced garlic

1 tablespoon minced ginger

1 cup diced onions

1 pound catfish filets

Method

Stir together all ingredients except catfish. Add catfish and marinate 1-24 hours. Preheat oven to 350.

Remove catfish from marinade and place on sheet pan. Top fish with marinated onions. Bake 20 minutes or until fish flakes in center.

Flounder With Almond

. . . .

Ingredients

½ cup sliced almonds toasted

½ cup butter

2 medium onions, thinly sliced

1 pound fresh or frozen flounder fillets, thawed

¾ cup mayonnaise

1 tablespoon chopped fresh parsley

Juice of 1 lemon

¼ cup shredded Parmesan cheese

Method

1. Preheat oven 350°.

2. Melt butter in shallow baking dish. Place onions on top of fish. In a small bowl, combine mayonnaise, parsley, and lemon juice. Spread evenly over fish. Sprinkle with cheese.

3. Bake 15 to 20 minutes, until fish flakes easily. Sprinkle with toasted almonds before serving.

Grilled Salmon With Lemon-Dill Sauce

Ingredients

Marinade

1 teaspoon canola or olive oil

1 tablespoon chopped fresh dill weed

1 teaspoon grated lemon peel

3 tablespoons lemon juice

2 tablespoons honey

½ teaspoon garlic-pepper blend

1 pound salmon fillets cut into 4 pieces (4 oz. each)

Lemon-Dill Sauce

1 container (6 oz.) Greek Fat Free plain yogurt

1 tablespoon chopped fresh dill weed or 1 teaspoon dried dill

½ teaspoon grated lemon peel

1 tablespoon lemon juice

1/8 teaspoon pepper

Method

1. In small bowl, mix all marinade ingredients except salmon.
2. In 8 inch square (2 quart) glass baking dish, arrange salmon pieces skin side up in single layer. Pour marinade over salmon; turn to coat. Cover with plastic wrap; refrigerate 20 minutes.
3. Heat gas or charcoal grill. Brush grill rack with oil. Remove salmon from marinade; discard marinade. Place skin side down on grill over medium heat. Cover grill; cook 10 to 15 minutes or until salmon flakes easily with fork.
4. Meanwhile, in small bowl, mix sauce ingredients. Serve with salmon.

Haddock Clam Chowder

Ingredients

4 strips bacon

3 tablespoons sliced green onions

2 celery ribs, chopped

2 cups diced peel potatoes

1 can (14-1/2 oz.) chicken broth

1 teaspoon dill weed

1 teaspoon celery seed, crushed

1-1/4 teaspoon salt

¼ teaspoon pepper

3 cups milk, divided

3 tablespoons all-purpose flour

2-1/2cups cubed cooked haddock

1 cup whipping cream

1 package (10 oz.) frozen chopped spinach, thawed

1 can (6-1/2 oz.) minced clams

Method

In a large saucepan, cook bacon until crisp. Place on paper towel. In the drippings, sauté onions and celery for 6 minutes or until crisp and tender. Add the potatoes, broth, dill, celery seed, salt and pepper. Bring to a boil. Reduce heat; cover and simmer for 20 minutes or until potatoes are tender. Add 2-½ cups of milk.

Combine flour and remaining milk; stir into soup. Bring to a boil; cook and stir for 3 minutes or until thickened. Add the haddock, cream, spinach and clams. Cook and stir until heated through. Garnish with bacon. Yield: 8 servings.

Healthy Shrimp Pasta

Ingredients

1 tablespoon olive oil

1 pound shrimp

1 ½ teaspoon paprika

2 teaspoons salt

½ teaspoon ground black pepper

½ cup onion

½ cup red pepper

1 tablespoon garlic

¼ cup smoked turkey

1-12 oz. can nonfat evaporated milk

2 teaspoons lemon juice

¼ cup finely chopped green onion

¼ cup Parmesan cheese

2 tablespoons parsley

1 pound whole-wheat fettuccine cooked

(According to directions on package)

Method

In a large skillet over medium heat, add olive oil. Season shrimp in a bowl with 1½ teaspoon paprika, 2 teaspoons salt, and ½ teaspoon black pepper.

Pour shrimp into skillet and sauté for 1½ minutes. Turn shrimp over and cook for 2 minutes. Remove shrimp from skillet and set aside.

Add ½ cup onion, ½ cup bell pepper and 1 tablespoon garlic and sauté for 3-4 minutes, stirring occasionally. Mix in ¼ cup smoked turkey and stir for 1 minute. Stir in evaporated milk, lemon juice, salt and pepper.

Bring ingredients to a boil and stir for 3 minutes until milk has slightly thickened. Return shrimp to pan, and stir for 2-1/2 minutes. Stir in ¼ cup green onion, cheese and parsley and stir ingredients to combine.

Add cooked pasta and toss until fettuccine is coated with sauce. Remove from heat, and adjust seasoning. Garnish with crushed red pepper to taste, and serve immediately. Yield: Makes 4 servings.

Lemony Stuffed Sole Fillets

. . . .

Ingredients

½ cup butter or margarine

1/3 cup chopped parsley

2 tablespoons chopped onion

1 cup herb seasoned stuffing mix

1 tablespoon chopped parsley

1 tablespoon lemon juice

1 teaspoon grated lemon peel

¼ teaspoon salt

¼ teaspoon pepper

1 pound sole or other fish fillets (4 medium)

¼ cup butter or margarine

½ teaspoon dill weed

Method

Preheat oven 350 degrees F. In one quart saucepan, melt 1/3 cup butter over medium heat. Add celery and onion, sauté until tender. Stir stuffing mix, parsley, lemon juice and peel, salt and pepper. Set aside.

Cut each fillet to make eight 3 X 4 inch halves. Place 4 halves in ungreased 9 inch square pan. Top each with 1/3 cup stuffing mixture; then remaining filet halves.

Melt 1/3 cup butter, stir in dill weed. Pour dill butter over filets. Bake at 350 degrees F for 20-30 minutes or until fish flakes with a fork. Spoon sauce over filets and serve with rice or a baked potato.

Poisson en Blaff

· ·

This peppery dish of poached fish is a popular dish from the islands of Martinique, Guadeloupe, St. Lucia, where it is often cooked right on the beach with freshly caught fish. The word "blaff" is said to come from the sound the fish makes when it hits the poaching liquid in the skillet.

Ingredients

3 cups water

5 tablespoons lime or lemon juice

1 fresh hot pepper, seeded and crushed

4 garlic cloves, minced

2 teaspoon salt

2 pounds red snappers, cleaned and scaled,

backbone removed, washed and ready to cook

1 cup dry white wine

1 large onion, finely chopped

1 whole fresh hot pepper

2 cloves

½ teaspoon allspice

1 bay leaf

1 teaspoon dried thyme

Method

Combine two cups of water with 4 tablespoons of the lime or lemon juice, 1 seeded and crushed fresh hot pepper, 3 of the minced garlic cloves, and the salt in a dish deep enough to hold the fish. Add the fish. Cover and marinate for 1 hour at room temperature.

Drain the fish and discard the marinade. Combine the wine, the remaining 1 cup water, onion, whole fresh hot pepper, remaining minced garlic clove, remaining 1 tablespoon lime or lemon juice, the cloves, allspice, bay leaf, and thyme in a large skillet. Bring to a boil, reduce the heat, and simmer for 5 minutes. Add the fish and continue to simmer for about 10 minutes.

Serve the fish with some of the poaching liquid with boiled green bananas and/or white rice and fried plantains. Serve with a vegetable salad on a side to complete the meal.

Salmon Patties

Ingredients

½ yellow onion, chopped

2 eggs, beaten

½ cup fine dried bread crumbs

¼ cup finely chopped fresh parsley

Salt and ground black pepper

1 pound cooked salmon fillet or

Canned salmon, picked over for bones and flaked

¼ cup cornmeal

3-4 tablespoons vegetable oil

Method

In a bowl, combine the onion, eggs, breadcrumbs, parsley, salt and pepper to taste, and salmon and mix lightly. Using your hands, form into 3 inch patties about ½ inch thick. Place the cornmeal on a shallow plate and dredge the patties in it.

In a heavy skillet, warm the oil over medium high heat. Add the patties and fry, turning once, until heated through and browned, 3-4 minutes on each side. Serve piping hot.

These patties are typically made with canned salmon stretched with breadcrumbs. A squeeze of fresh lemon juice or a little yellow mustard spread on top is just the right condiment for the canned salmon version.

Salmon With Chive Mayonnaise

Ingredients

½ cup mayonnaise

3 tablespoons white wine or chicken broth

¼ cup minced chives

1 tablespoon minced fresh thyme

1 teaspoon snipped fresh dill or 1 teaspoon dill weed

1/8 teaspoon pepper

2 salmon steaks (3/4 inch thick)

Method

In a bowl, combine the first six ingredients; set aside 1/3 cup for serving. Place salmon steaks on a broiler rack. Broil 4 inches from the heat for nine minutes. Brush with remaining mayonnaise mixture. Turn salmon over; broil 9 minutes longer or until fish flakes easily with a fork. Serve with reserved mayonnaise mixture. Serves 2

Salmon with Red Cabbage

. . . .

Ingredients

4 5-ounce fillets fresh or frozen salmon

¼ cup balsamic vinegar

¼ teaspoon kosher or sea salt or ¼ teaspoon salt

¼ teaspoon black pepper

¼ cup prepared basil pesto

6 cups coarsely shredded red cabbage

2 green onions, sliced

Method

1. Thaw salmon, if frozen. Place salmon fillets on greased unheated rack of broiler pan. Measure thickness of salmon. Brush salmon with 1 tablespoon of the balsamic vinegar; sprinkle salmon with salt and pepper. Broil salmon 4 to 5 inches from heat for 4 to 6 minutes per ½ inch thickness or until salmon flakes easily with a fork.

2. Meanwhile, in bowl whisk together remaining vinegar and pesto until combined. Remove 2 tablespoons pesto mixture. Add cabbage to pesto mixture in bowl; toss to coat.

3. To serve, place cabbage mixture on plate; top with salmon. Drizzle with reserved pesto mixture. Sprinkle with green onion slices.

Seafood Minestrone

Ingredients

2 cloves garlic, minced

1 tablespoon extra virgin olive oil

2 leeks, halved lengthwise and sliced ½ inch thick

2 14-oz. cans reduced sodium chicken broth

2 cups water

1 15-oz. can navy beans, rinsed and drained

1 teaspoon dried thyme, crushed

4 ounces broken dry linguini or fettuccini

1 pound peeled and deveined medium shrimp and/or bay scallop

4 medium Roma tomatoes, coarsely chopped

1 cup fresh spinach

Freshly ground pepper

Method

In 4 quart Dutch oven, cook garlic in oil for 15 seconds; add leeks. Cook and stir until tender. Add broth, water, beans, and thyme; bring to boiling. Add linguini. Simmer, uncovered, for 10 to 12 minutes or until pasta is tender, stirring occasionally. Stir in seafood. Simmer for 2 minutes or until seafood is just opaque. Divide among soup plates. Add tomatoes and spinach. Season to taste with pepper. Makes 4 servings.

Stir Fry Sweet and Sour Shrimp

Ingredients

1 12-oz. package frozen peeled, deveined shrimp

1/3 cup bottled stir fry sauce

¼ cup pineapple-orange, orange, or apple juice

Nonstick cooking spray

3 cups assorted fresh stir fry vegetables

Method

1. Thaw shrimp, rinse and pat dry with paper towels. Set aside. In a small bowl combine stir fry sauce and juice.

2. Coat an unheated nonstick wok or large skillet with nonstick cooking spray. (Add oil during cooking, if necessary). Preheat wok over medium high heat. Add vegetables; stir fry for 3 to 5 minutes or until crisp tender. Remove vegetables from wok. Add shrimp; stir fry for 2 to 3 minutes or until shrimp are opaque. Push shrimp to side of wok.

3. Add sauce mixture to wok. Return vegetables to wok. Toss gently to coat. Cook and stir about 1 minute more or until heated through.

Makes 4 servings

Walleye in Batter

Feel Free To Substitute Your Favorite Fish

Ingredients

1 cup biscuit/baking mix

1 tablespoon garlic powder

1 tablespoon onion powder

1 tablespoon Cajun seasoning

1½ teaspoon pepper

1 teaspoon salt

½ cup 2% milk

Oil for frying

1 pound walleye fillets, skin removed

Lemon wedges

Method

1. In a shallow bowl, mix the first six ingredients. Place milk in a separate shallow bowl. In an electric skillet, heat ¼ inch oil to 375 degrees.

2. In batches, dip fish in milk, then coat with baking mix mixture, fry for 5 minutes on each side or until golden brown and fish flakes easily with a fork. Serve immediately with lemon wedges.

Side Dish

Baked Green Bananas

Ingredients

6 green (unripe) bananas cooked and mashed

2 tablespoons butter or margarine, at room temperature

1 small hot pepper, seeded and minced

1 scallion, finely chopped

½ teaspoon dried thyme

1 cup milk

1 small onion, chopped

1 tablespoon fresh parsley leaves

Salt to taste

Method

Peel bananas with a knife and boil in water for 20 minutes or until soft.

Cream the bananas with butter until smooth, then add the hot pepper, scallion, thyme, and milk. Stir; add the onion, parsley, and salt to taste, mixing well.

Turn into a well buttered 2 quart casserole, and bake in a preheated 350o F oven for about 20 minutes, or until the top is brown. Serve hot as a side dish directly from the casserole.

Serves 6

Baked Sweet Potato Fries

Ingredients

Nonstick cooking spray

1 pound medium sweet potatoes

1 tablespoon margarine or butter, melted

¼ teaspoon seasoned salt

Dash nutmeg

Method

1. Lightly coat a 15x10x1 inch cookie sheet with cooking spray.
2. Scrub potatoes; cut lengthwise into quarters. Cut each quarter into two wedges.
3. Arrange potatoes in a single layer in pan.
4. Combine margarine or butter, salt, and nutmeg.
5. Brush onto potatoes. Bake in a 425° degree oven for 20 to 30 minutes or until brown and tender. Makes 4 servings.

Bean Pot Dinner

Ingredients

1 can green limas, drained

1 can kidney beans, drained

1 can Garbanzo beans, drained

1 can butter beans (undrained)

1 can pork and beans (undrained)

½ pound hamburger

½ pound diced bacon

1 large onion

Sauce

½ cup ketchup

½ cup barbecue sauce

3 tablespoons vinegar

1 teaspoon dry mustard

1 teaspoon chili powder

Couple dashes of Worcestershire sauce

Simmer sauce for 15 minutes

Method

Mix the beans together. Sauté hamburger with onion and drain. Add to beans. Sauté bacon; drain and add to beans (can add a couple tablespoons of the bacon grease). Stir in the sauce and bake for one hour at 350 degrees; or cook on low in crock pot all day. Serve with hot dogs or with crackers or fresh bread.

Broccoli and Ham Quiche

Ingredients

1 box refrigerated pie crust, softened as directed on box

1½ cups cubed (1/4 inch) cooked ham

1½ cups shredded Swiss cheese (6 oz.)

1 cup frozen broccoli florets, thawed, well drained on paper towel

4 eggs

1 cup milk

½ teaspoon salt

½ teaspoon dry ground mustard

½ teaspoon pepper

Method

1. Heat oven to 375°F. Place pie crust in 9 inch glass pie pan as directed on box for one filled pie.

2. Layer ham, cheese and broccoli in crust lined pan. In medium bowl, beat eggs and milk with fork. Stir in salt, ground mustard and pepper. Pour over broccoli.

3. Bake 35 to 45 minutes or until knife inserted in center comes out clean. Let stand 5 to 10 minutes before serving.

Butternut Squash *and* Apple Bake

. . . .

This is so good you could almost serve it for dessert. It has an apple pie flavor with fresh apples on the bottom and covered with mashed butternut squash. Top it with cereal and nuts and you have a side dish with lots of vitamin A, beta-carotene, and fiber.

2 medium apples, peeled and cored
2 tablespoon cinnamon sugar mixture

Topping
1 cup corn flakes, slightly crushed
1/4 cup chopped pecans
1 tablespoon brown sugar
1 tablespoon butter, melted

Ingredients

1 medium (1 1/2 pounds) butternut squash
1 tablespoon butter or margarine
1 tablespoon brown sugar
Salt and pepper to taste

Method

Microwave squash for 4 – 5 minutes or just enough to soften slightly. (The squash will be easier and safer to cut when softened). Peel squash and cut in half lengthwise. Remove seeds and cut into chunks. Place in a large pan with 2 inches of water. Cover and steam for 20 - 30 minutes or until squash is tender. Drain well. Add 1 tablespoon butter and brown sugar. Mash with electric mixer. Add salt and pepper to taste. Set aside.

Preheat oven to 350 degrees. Heavily butter a deep 9 inch pie pan. Thinly slice apples and arrange in pan. Sprinkle with cinnamon and sugar mixture. Spread mashed squash over apples.

In a small bowl, combine topping ingredients. Sprinkle over squash.

Bake for 30-40 minutes, or until apples are tender. Serves 8

Cassava Pone

Ingredients

- 2 pounds sweet cassava
- 1 mature coconut
- ½ teaspoon grated nutmeg
- 5-6 drops vanilla essence
- 6 oz. raw cane sugar
- 1 pint milk

Method

Peel and grate the cassava and coconut. Combine in a bowl with grated nutmeg, vanilla essence and sugar. Stir in the milk to form a soft thick batter. Pour the mixture into a well greased baking dish and bake in a preheated oven at 180 degrees for 1¼ hour or until set.

Serves 6

This recipe requires a bit of effort in grating the two main ingredients, the cassava and coconut, but the end result is well worth the time involved.

Cheesy Margarita Pizza

Ingredients

1 can 8 oz. refrigerated dinner rolls

2 teaspoons olive oil

1½ cups shredded mozzarella cheese blend

6 ounces

3 medium plum Roma tomatoes, sliced

2 tablespoons fresh basil strips (may use dried basil)

Method

Separate or cut dough into two long rectangles, press perforations to seal. Place on ungreased cookie sheet, press into 12 X 8 inch rectangle. Brush with oil.

Top with cheese and tomatoes.

Bake at 375o F for 12 to 15 minutes. Sprinkle with basil.

Cinnamon Toast Blueberry Bakes

Ingredients

4 slices whole wheat bread

6 tablespoons melted butter

3 tablespoons sugar

½ teaspoon cinnamon

1 cup fresh or frozen blueberries

¼ cup packed brown sugar

2 teaspoons lemon juice

Method

1. Cut 4 slices of whole wheat bread into ½ inch pieces and place in a large bowl. Combine 6 tablespoons melted butter, 3 tablespoons sugar and ½ teaspoon ground cinnamon. Drizzle over bread. Toss and coat.

2. Combine 1 cup fresh or frozen blueberries, ¼ cup packed brown sugar and 2 teaspoons lemon juice. Place half of the bread mixture into four individual baking dishes. Layer with blueberry mixture and remaining bread. Bake, uncovered at 350 degrees for 15-20 minutes or until crisp and heated through. Makes 4 servings.

Collard Greens

Ingredients

3 quarts water

½ pound smoked meat (smoked turkey wings, ham hocks, or smoked neck bones)

1 tablespoon house dressing, recipe follows

1 tablespoon seasoned salt

1 tablespoon hot red pepper sauce

1 large bunch collard greens

1 tablespoon butter

Method

In a large pan, bring three quarts of water to a boil and add smoked meat, house seasoning, seasoned salt and hot sauce. Reduce heat to medium and cook for 1 hour.

Wash the collard greens thoroughly. Remove the stems that run down the center by holding the leaf in your left hand and stripping the leaf down with your right hand. The tender young leaves in the heart of the collards don't need to be stripped. Stack 6 to 8 leaves on top of one another, roll up, and slice into ½ to 1 inch thick slices. Place greens in pot with meat and add butter. Cook for 2 hours till tender, stirring occasionally. When done, taste and adjust seasoning.

House Seasoning

½ cup black pepper

¼ cup garlic powder

Serve as a side dish with your favorite dish.

Corn Bread Dressing

Ingredients

1 yellow onion chopped

4 green onions, including tops, chopped

2 celery stalks, chopped

6 cups corn bread cubes

2 teaspoon ground sage or dried sage leaves, crushed

½ cup fresh chopped parsley

2 eggs lightly beaten

¼ cup butter melted

Salt and ground black pepper

1-1/2 cups chicken or turkey stock

Method

Preheat oven to 375 degrees F. Butter a 4 quart baking dish if not using to stuff a turkey.

In a large bowl, combine all the ingredients, except the stock, seasoning to taste with salt and pepper. Mix well. Pour enough stock to achieve desired moistness and mix well. If stuffing the mixture into a turkey, use the smaller amount of stock.

Put the dressing in the prepared baking dish or stuff the bird. Cover and bake for 30 minutes. Uncover and bake until it just begins to brown on top, another 30 minutes. Serve hot.

Corn Porridge

Ingredients

8 oz. hominy corn

1 pint water

1 pint coconut milk

2 tablespoon corn flour

1 stick of cinnamon

½ teaspoon freshly grated nutmeg

½ tablespoon rosewater

raw cane sugar

Method

Wash the corn, place in a pan with the water and boil until soft. Mix the coconut milk with the corn flour and pour into the pan. Cook stirring continuously as the mixture thickens. Add the spices and rosewater and simmer for 15-20 minutes, giving the porridge an occasional stir. Sweeten to taste with raw cane sugar.

Serves 4

Eggplant and Tomato Parmesan

. . . .

This is a fresh and tasty side dish to serve along with meat or poultry.

Ingredients

2 small eggplants, cut crosswise
6 medium plum tomatoes, cut crosswise
into ¼ inch slices
1 teaspoon salt
¼ teaspoon freshly ground black pepper
2 tablespoons extra virgin olive oil
2 cloves garlic, minced
6 to 8 basil leaves, finely chopped,
Or about 1 teaspoon dried leaf basil
Fresh shredded Parmesan cheese

Method

Spray a large shallow baking pan with olive oil spray or grease with olive oil. Heat oven to 425 degrees.

In a large food storage bag or bowl, toss the sliced eggplant and tomatoes with the salt, pepper, olive oil, garlic, and basil.

Spread the sliced tomatoes and eggplant out in the prepared baking pan in a single layer (overlapping a little is okay, but if you're stacking, use 2 pans).

Bake the slices for 35 minutes, or until vegetables are nicely browned. Sprinkle with fresh Parmesan cheese. Serves 4 to 6.

Flour Dumplings

. . . .

There are many varieties of dumplings; the flour dumplings is the most popular in the Caribbean and simplest to make

Ingredients

1 cup all purpose flour
¼ teaspoon salt
Water

Method

Sift the flour and salt into a bowl and slowly add enough cold water to make a stiff dough. (A sticky dough makes a soft pastry dumpling). Knead in a bowl or on a lightly floured board until smooth. Shape into small balls that fit in the palm of your hand and flatten in the palm of one hand by using karate like chops with the other hand.

Immerse into salted boiling water and cook for 15 to 20 minutes. Can also add to soups and stews and cook for the same period or longer. Yield: 6 to 9 dumplings

Fried Okra

Ingredients

- ½ cup cornmeal
- 1 cup all purpose flour
- 1 teaspoon garlic powder
- 1 teaspoon cayenne pepper
- 2 pounds fresh okra, sliced ½ inch thick
- ½ cup buttermilk
- 2 teaspoons salt
- 6 cups oil, for frying

Method

Heat oil in a large heavy skillet. You may not need to use all the oil, do not fill the pan with oil – just enough to brown the okra.

In a medium bowl, combine cornmeal, flour, salt, and cayenne pepper. Dip okra in buttermilk and then coat in cornmeal flour mixture. Add okra to the hot oil and cook until golden brown. Remove from oil, drain on paper towels and serve immediately.

Garlic-Chive Baked Fries

Ingredients

4 medium Russet potatoes, cut into 1 inch julienne strips

1 tablespoon olive oil

4 teaspoon dried minced chives

½ teaspoon salt

½ teaspoon garlic powder

¼ teaspoon pepper

Method

1. Cut potatoes into 1 inch strips. Rinse well and pat dry.

2. Drizzle with one tablespoon olive oil, and sprinkle with 4 teaspoon dried minced chives, ½ teaspoon salt, ½ teaspoon garlic powder and ¼ teaspoon pepper. Toss to coat.

3. Arrange in a single layer on two 15-inch x10-inch x 1 inch baking pan coated with cooking spray.

4. Bake at 450° for 20-25 minutes or until lightly browned, turning once. Makes 4 servings.

Potato Parsnip Pancakes

. . . .

Ingredients

2/3 cup light olive oil, for frying
3 medium potatoes, peeled and shredded
1 small parsnip, peeled and grated
1 small onion, peeled
1 egg, beaten
1 tablespoon parsley
1 tablespoon chives, finely sliced
1 tablespoon dill
3 tablespoons all-purpose flour, or cracker meal
Salt and pepper

Method

Heat about 1/3 cup oil over medium heat.

Drain the shredded potatoes and parsnip, pressing them down in a colander to remove the moisture.

Place the mixture in a bowl; using a box grater, grate the onion directly into the potato mixture so the onion juices fall into the bowl as well.

Add the egg, parsley, chives, dill and flour to the bowl and season with salt and pepper.

Combine and drop enough batter into hot oil to made 2 ½ inch pancakes.

Add more oil, as needed and fry cakes in batches until deeply golden on each side.

Roasted Eggplant and Tomatoes With Parmesan Cheese

. . . .

Ingredients

2 small eggplants, cut crosswise into ¼ inch slices

6 medium plum tomatoes, cut into ¼ inch slices

1 teaspoon salt

¼ teaspoon freshly ground black pepper

2 tablespoons extra virgin olive oil

2 cloves garlic, minced

1 teaspoon dried leaf basil

Fresh shredded Parmesan cheese

Method

Spray a large shallow baking pan with olive oil spray. Heat oven at 425°F.

In a large food storage bag, toss the sliced eggplant and tomatoes with salt, pepper, olive oil, garlic and basil.

Spread the sliced tomatoes and eggplant out in the prepared baking pan in a single layer. Bake the slices for 35 to 45 minutes, or until vegetables are nicely browned. Sprinkle with Parmesan cheese.

Shrimp Risotto Recipe

. . . .

Ingredients

2 tablespoons olive oil

Salt and pepper

2 cloves garlic, chopped fine

1 cup dry white wine

½ pound baby carrots, blanched

3 tablespoons olive oil

1 pound rice

4 cups chicken stock

½ cup basil leaves, cut in strips

4 tablespoons cold butter

2 pounds jumbo shrimp

1 shallot, chopped fine

5 plum tomatoes seeded and diced

2 tablespoons cold butter

1/2 pound snap peas blanched

1 onion, diced

½ cup dry white wine

4 tomatoes, seeded and diced

½ cup Parmesan cheese grated

Salt and pepper

Method

Heat stockpot over medium high heat. Add olive oil, onion and sauté for 4 to 5 minutes. Add rice and cook for 3 minutes. Add wine and cook for 5 minutes. Add stock 1 cup at a time, stirring constantly. Cook for 20 minutes or until just cooked. Add remaining ingredients, set aside and keep warm.

Heat sauté pan over medium high heat. Add 2 tablespoons olive oil. Season shrimp with salt and pepper and add to the pan. Cook for 2 to 3 minutes on each side and add shallot, garlic, tomatoes, and wine and cook for 3 more minutes. Add butter 1 piece at a time, and season with salt and pepper. Sauté carrots and green beans in butter. Divide rice among 4 plates. Top with shrimp and pour sauce over and enjoy.

Southwest Cornbread Casserole

Ingredients

1 cup cornmeal

1 cup milk

1 can 13 oz. cream style corn

¾ teaspoon salt

1 teaspoon baking powder

2 beaten eggs

¼ cup oil

1 large onion

1 pound ground beef or cooked shredded chicken

1 packet taco seasoning

8 oz. shredded jack or cheddar cheese

Method

Mix together cornmeal, milk, corn, eggs, baking powder, salt and oil to make batter. Simmer the meat with taco seasoning, per package directions. Pour half the batter into a greased 2 quart baking dish. Layer meat, onion, and cheese, then pour remaining batter on top. Bake at 350° for 40-50 minutes until browned and crusty on top. Serve with beans, salsa and sour cream

Spicy Caribbean Risotto With Citrus Chicken

Ingredients

For the risotto

½ red onion, finely chopped

1 tablespoon olive oil

1 tablespoon butter

¼ teaspoon ground cardamom

½ teaspoon chili flakes

1 cube vegetable stock, crumbled

Salt and freshly ground black pepper

1 carrot, peeled and grated

½ cup risotto rice

½ teaspoon coriander seeds

½ teaspoon dried turmeric

½ cup white wine

1 garlic clove, finely chopped

For the chicken

1 skinless chicken breast, flattened with a rolling pin

Zest of 1 lime

Zest of 1 orange

Lime wedges, to garnish

Method

1. For the risotto, heat the oil in a deep frying pan. Fry the onion, carrot, rice and the butter until coated.

2. Grind the coriander seeds in a pestle or food processor and add the other dry spices and chili flakes. Add to the rice.

3. Add the wine and stir well to deglaze the pan.

4. Add the cube stock and garlic and stir well.

5. Begin adding ¾ cup hot water gradually, a little at a time until the rice is cooked through.

6. Meanwhile, heat a griddle pan for the chicken.

7. Toss the chicken breast in the lime and orange zest. Place on the griddle and grill for three minutes on each side or until cooked through. Remove from the heat and leave to stand for two minutes.

8. Slice the chicken breast and serve on top of the risotto with the lime wedge to garnish.

Spoon Bread

. . . .

Ingredients

4 slices bacon

1 cup water

½ cup yellow cornmeal

1/2 cup shredded cheddar cheese (4 ounces)

1 8.75 oz. can cream style corn

2 tablespoons margarine or butter

¼ teaspoon onion powder

Dash of garlic powder

¾ cup milk

3 egg yolks

1 teaspoon baking powder

3 egg whites

Method

1. Cook bacon until crisp, drain and crumble. Set bacon aside.

2. In a medium saucepan, combine water and cornmeal; bring to boil. Reduce heat, cook and stir until very thick. Remove from heat. Stir in cheese, corn, margarine, onion powder, and garlic powder. Stir until cheese melts and mixture is smooth. Stir in milk.

3. In a small mixing bowl beat egg yolks and baking powder until well blended. Stir into cornmeal mixture along with bacon.

4. In a medium mixing bowl, beat egg whites until stiff peaks form.

5. Fold beaten egg whites into cornmeal. Pour into a lightly greased 1½ quart casserole. Bake at 325o F oven for 50 to 60 minutes until a knife inserted near the center comes out clean. Serve immediately. Makes 6 servings.

Sweet Bean Pilaf

Ingredients

- 1 medium onion, chopped
- 2 cloves garlic, minced
- 1 tablespoon olive oil
- 1 cup orange juice
- 1 cup chicken broth
- 1 cup bulgur
- 1 cup soybeans
- 1 medium carrot, cut into thin bite strips
- 1 stalk celery, bias sliced
- 1/3 dried tart cherries
- 2 oranges, peeled and sectioned

Method

1. Cook onion and garlic in hot oil in a saucepan until onion is tender.
2. Stir in orange juice, broth, bulgur, soybeans, carrot, and celery.
3. Bring to boiling; reduce heat. Simmer, covered, for 10 to 12 minutes or until soybeans are tender and liquid is absorbed.
4. Stir in cherries or raisins and orange sections.

Makes 4 servings

Sweet Potato Casserole

. . . .

Ingredients

6 pounds dark orange sweet potatoes (9 large or 12 medium)

8 oz. bacon (8 to 10 slices)

¼ cup crispy breadcrumbs or plain bread crumbs

1 tablespoon butter or margarine, melted

½ cup sour cream

¼ cup butter or margarine, softened

2 medium green onions, chopped (2 tablespoons)

½ teaspoon salt

¼ teaspoon pepper

Method

1. Heat oven to 350°F. Line and spray 13x9 inch (3 quart) glass baking dish with cooking spray. Pierce sweet potatoes several times with fork. Place in flat dish. Cook in microwave for about 15 minutes or until tender. Cool 10 minutes. When potatoes are cool enough to handle, use a spoon to scrape out cooked potatoes.

2. Meanwhile, cook bacon as desired until crisp; chop. In small bowl, mix breadcrumbs and 1 tablespoon butter; set aside.

3. In large bowl, mash potatoes with potato masher. Stir in chopped bacon, sour cream, ¼ cup butter, the onions, salt and pepper until well blended. Spread mixture in baking dish, or form individual servings in dish with 1/2-cup ice cream scoop or measuring cup. Sprinkle crumb mixture evenly over top.

4. Bake 20 to 30 minutes or until thoroughly heated and bread crumbs just begin to brown. Save prep time by using precooked bacon.

This casserole can be made the day before. Simply cover it and refrigerate until you're ready to bake.

Sweet Potato Pone

This particular pone, similar to those found in the Southern part of the United States, was inspired by the rich culinary heritage of Africa.

Ingredients

2 pounds sweet potatoes, peeled and sliced

2 tablespoons brown sugar

2 tablespoons butter

¼ cup orange juice

2 large eggs

½ cup dark rum

¼ teaspoon salt

Method

1. Cook the sweet potatoes in boiling water for 20 minutes until tender. Drain and mash the potatoes with the brown sugar and butter. Stir in the orange juice. Lightly beat the egg yolks and add them to the sweet potato mixture along with the rum.

2. Preheat the oven to 350°F. Grease a pie plate or baking dish and set it aside.

3. Beat the egg white with the salt until stiff but not dry. Gently fold the egg whites into the potato mixture. Pour into the prepared dish and bake for 30 minutes until a knife inserted in the center comes out clean.

Serves 6-8. Preparation time: 10 mins. Cooking time: 50 mins.

Vegetable Fried Rice

Ingredients

1 tablespoon toasted sesame oil

2 teaspoons fresh or bottled minced garlic

2 teaspoons fresh or bottled minced ginger

3 cups mixed cut up fresh vegetables (packed or from the salad bar) such as sweet pepper, red onion, sliced mushrooms, broccoli florets, or thin baby carrots

1-1/2 cups coarsely chopped bok choy

3 cups cold cooked or brown rice

¼ cup reduced sodium soy sauce

2 teaspoons thinly sliced green onion (1) or snipped fresh cilantro (optional)

Method

1. In a 12 inch nonstick skillet, heat sesame oil over medium heat. Add garlic and ginger; cook and stir for 1 minute. Add mixed vegetables and bok choy; cook and stir for 3 to 4 minutes or until vegetables are crisp tender. Add rice and soy sauce; cook and stir for 3 minutes. If desired, sprinkle with green onion. Makes 8 side dish servings.

2. **Note:** For a main dish for four, add 2 cups diced cooked chicken or shrimp with the rice and soy sauce.

Soups

Beef Barley Soup

Ingredients

2 pounds ground round

2 medium onions, chopped

½ cup chopped celery

3 cups water

2 cans (14-1/2 ounces each beef broth)

1 cup quick cooking barley

2 cans (14-1/2 ounces each diced tomatoes with garlic and onion, undrained

2 tablespoons Worcestershire sauce

1 teaspoon salt

1 teaspoon dried basil

Method

1. Cook beef, onions, and celery until meat is no longer pink and vegetables are tender; drain.

2. Stir in the water and broth; bring to a boil. Reduce heat.

3. Add barley, cover and simmer for 20 minutes or until tender. Stir in the remaining ingredients; heat through. Transfer to 1 quart freezer containers; cover and freeze for up to 3 months.

4. To use frozen soup: Thaw in the refrigerator; place in a saucepan and heat through. Makes 3 batches (3 quarts total).

Beef Tortellini Soup

Ingredients

1 can (14.5 oz.) diced tomatoes, undrained
1 pound beef stew meat
1 large onion, chopped (3/4 cup)
1 large carrot, chopped (3/4 cup)
1 medium stalk celery, chopped (1/2 cup)
2 cloves garlic, finely chopped
2 teaspoons sugar
2½ cups beef flavored broth (from 32 ounces carton)
1 teaspoon dried basil leaves
2 cups frozen cheese filled tortellini
1 cup frozen cut green beans

Method

Spray 3-1/2- to 4-quart slow cooker with cooking spray. Add beef, onion, carrot, celery, garlic, sugar, tomatoes and broth to cooker in order listed.

Cover; cook on low heat setting 8 to 9 hours.

About 25 minutes before serving, stir in basil, frozen tortellini and green beans. Increase heat setting to High. Cover and cook about 25 minutes or until beans are tender. Makes 6 servings

Dr. Oz Belly Blasting Soup

· ·

Ingredients

1 (14.5 oz.) can of fire roasted tomatoes with medium chilies

1 (15 oz.) can chickpeas

2 cloves garlic chopped

2 cups vegetable or chicken broth

2 tablespoons chili powder

¼ cup limejuice

½ cup chopped cilantro

Method

1. Puree the tomatoes, chickpeas and garlic with the broth and chili powder in a blender (in batches, if necessary). Transfer mix to a medium large pot, bring to a boil, lower the heat and simmer for about 10 minutes. (If using a blender, you can process the ingredients directly in the cooking pot).

2. Before serving, stir in the juice and cilantro. Enjoy.

Makes 4-1/2 cups

Butternut Squash Soup II

Ingredients

2 tablespoons margarine or butter

½ cup chopped onion

1 (2 pounds) butternut squash, peeled, cubed

2 cups water

½ teaspoon dried marjoram leaves

¼ teaspoon coarsely ground black pepper

1/8 teaspoon ground red pepper (cayenne)

4 chicken flavor bouillon cubes

1 (8 oz.) packet cream cheese, cubed

Method

1. Melt margarine in large skillet over medium heat. Add onion; cook until crisp tender, stirring occasionally.

2. In a slow cooker, combine onion and all remaining ingredients except cream cheese; mix well.

3. Cover; cook on low setting for 6 to 8 hours.

4. About 40 minutes before serving, place about 1/3 of mixture at a time into blender container or food processor bowl with metal blade. Cover; blend or process on high speed until smooth. Return mixture to slow cooker.

5. Stir in cream cheese. Cover; cook on low setting an additional 30 minutes or until cheese is melted, stirring with wire whisk until smooth.

For a chunky veggie version of this soup, stir in a 1-pound package of frozen mixed vegetables (thawed and drained) with the cream cheese.

Butternut Squash Soup

Ingredients

Roasted Winter Squash

2 teaspoon butter

2 cups diced (3/4 inch) raw winter squash

(Butternut, Hubbard, acorn)

Salt and pepper

Soup

2 tablespoons extra virgin olive oil

½ cup diced onion (1/4 inch)

¼ cup diced celery

¼ cup diced carrot

1 cinnamon stick

Sea salt and freshly ground pepper

1 carton (32 oz.) chicken broth (4 cups)

½ teaspoon ground toasted coriander,

if desired

1 ½ roasted winter squash (above)

½ cup half-and-half, if desired

2 tablespoon toasted pumpkin seeds

½ cup plain crispy bread crumbs,

Toasted light brown in pan oven

medium heat

Method

To make roasted winter squash – heat oven to 375F. Melt butter over medium high heat in an ovenproof sauté pan; add diced squash, salt and pepper. When squash begins to brown, place pan in oven. Roast for 15 minutes or until medium-brown on all sides. Remove from oven and let cool slightly. Puree in food processor, or mash with potato masher. Measure 1 ½ cups squash, reserve.

To make soup: Heat the olive oil in a large saucepan over medium heat until hot. Add the onion, celery, carrot and cinnamon stick; sauté until soft but not brown for about 10 minutes. Season to taste with salt and pepper. Add the broth and the coriander; bring to a boil. Simmer for several minutes. Stir in reserved squash until smooth; simmer gently to let the flavors meld, about 10 minutes. Discard the cinnamon stick. Puree the soup using a blender until smooth. The soup can be made ahead of time can be refrigerated for several days or frozen for one month. May need thinning with broth or water when reheating.

Callaloo Soup With Spinach and Lentil and Dumplings

Ingredients

6 ¾ pounds *madere leaves or spinach

4 tablespoons sunflower oil

2 cloves garlic, chopped

2 onions chopped

2 sprigs flat leaf parsley, finely chopped

11 ounces *lardons (bacon bits)

Method

Bring one cup lightly salted water to boil in a Dutch oven or flameproof casserole. Immerse the madere leaves and cook for 10 minutes. Drain the leaves, reserve the cooking water, and immediately plunge the cooked leaves into ice water so they remain green. Drain, then puree in a blender or food processor.

Heat the oil in a heavy based saucepan then gently fry the garlic, onion and parsley without browning. Add the lardons and simmer for 2 minutes, stirring from time to time. Add the leaf puree and half the cooking water. Season to taste with salt and pepper. Cook over low heat for 5 minutes more. Serve hot.

Cauliflower Cheese Soup

· ·

Ingredients

1 small head cauliflower, cut into florets

1 tablespoon olive oil

1 onion, chopped

1 rib of celery, chopped

1 cup reduced sodium chicken broth

1 1/2 cups half-and-half

1/2 teaspoon dried thyme

½ teaspoon parsley

1/8 teaspoon ground black pepper

Pinch of ground nutmeg

1 1/2 cups shredded reduced fat white cheddar cheese (6 ounces)

1/4 teaspoon salt

Method

1. Bring a medium pot of water to a boil.
2. Set aside 12 bite-size cauliflower florets. Coarsely chop remaining cauliflower and set aside.
3. Drop the 12 florets in boiling water and blanch for 2 minutes. Drain and set aside.
4. Heat oil in a medium saucepan over medium heat. Add onion and celery, and cook until soft, about 5 minutes. Add chopped cauliflower, broth, half-and-half, thyme, parsley, pepper, and nutmeg.

5. Cover and simmer until cauliflower is tender. Puree the soup in a blender and return to the pot.

6. Stir in the cheese and salt until the cheese melts and the soup is heated through, 3 minutes.

7. Serve topped with cauliflower florets.

TIP: For a vegetarian soup, use vegetable broth instead of chicken broth.

Chicken and Dumplings

. . . .

Ingredients

1 large onion, cut into 1 inch dice

4 ribs celery, cut into ¼ inch slices

4 medium carrots, peeled and cut into ¼ inch slices

1 whole garlic clove, peeled

4 large sprigs fresh thyme

2 tablespoons extra virgin olive oil

3 quarts water

salt and freshly ground black pepper, to taste

1 large (about 5 pounds) chicken, quartered, or 5 pounds chicken legs and thighs

1 loaf country white bread, crusts removed and cut into ½ inch cubes

3 cups cold water

3 large eggs, beaten

paprika to taste

Method

In a large stockpot or dutch oven over medium heat, saute the onion, celery, carrots, garlic, and thyme in the oil for 7 to 10 minutes. Add the 3 quarts of water and season with salt and pepper. Add the chicken, bring to a simmer, and continue simmering 25 to 35 minutes, or until the chicken is cooked through.

Remove chicken from the pot while the broth continues to simmer and pull all of the meat off the bones. Return the meat to the pot while preparing the dumplings.

Soak the bread in the cold water for 1 minute. Squeeze as much water out of the bread as possible. In a medium bowl, work the eggs, paprika, and salt and pepper into the bread to form a dough.

Skim the fat off of the top of the broth with a spoon. Add the dumpling dough, one spoonful at a time, into the simmering soup. Cook 2 to 3 minutes, or until the dumplings float. Adjust seasoning and serve.

Chicken Tortilla Soup

. . . .

Ingredients

6 boneless skinless chicken thighs (1-1/4 pounds)

1 medium onion, chopped (1/2 cup)

3 (6 inch) corn tortillas, cut into 1 inch pieces

1½ cups frozen whole kernel corn, thawed

1 can (15 oz.) chickpeas or garbanzo beans, drained, rinsed

1 can (4.5 oz.) chopped green chiles

¾ cup salsa

2 cans (14 oz. each) chicken broth

1 teaspoon dried oregano leaves

1 teaspoon ground cumin

½ teaspoon ground red pepper (cayenne)

2 tomatoes, seeded, chopped

Chopped fresh cilantro leaves, if desired

Method

1. In 3 - to 4 quart crock pot, mix all ingredients except tomatoes and cilantro.

2. Cover and cook on low heat setting 5 to 7 hours or until juice of chicken is clear when center of thickest part is cut (250F). Stir to break up chicken thighs. Stir in tomatoes before serving. Garnish with cilantro.

Curried Pumpkin Soup

Ingredients

1 tablespoon canola oil

1 tablespoon butter

1 cup chopped onions

¾ cup chopped carrots

2 cloves garlic, minced

2 teaspoons minced fresh ginger

1½ teaspoons curry powder

1½ to 2 cups vegetable broth

2 cans (15 oz. each) 100 percent pumpkin puree

1 cup canned coconut milk

½ teaspoon salt

Pinch of sugar

Method

1. Heat oil and butter in large saucepan over medium heat until hot. Add onion, carrot, garlic, ginger, and curry powder. Cook until carrots are soft, 5 to 8 minutes.

2. Pour in 1-1/2 cups of broth and bring to a boil over high heat. Reduce heat to medium/low, cover and simmer for 10 minutes. Stir in pumpkin, coconut milk, salt, and sugar, and cook 2 minutes. Transfer to a blender or food processor and puree until very smooth.

3. Return to pan and heat through. Served with the toasted slices of bread.

TIP: For a nice presentation, put a dollop of sour cream in the center of each bowl and scatter on some minced red bell pepper and cilantro.

Fisherman's Soup

Ingredients

1 medium size lobster, cooked or ½ pound cooked lobster meat

¼ pound raw shrimp with shells

½ pound white fleshed fish fillet

6 cups chicken stock

1 onion, sliced

2 potatoes, peeled and sliced

2 bay leaves, crumbled

2 garlic cloves

2 tablespoons tomato paste

2 large tomatoes, seeded and chopped

¼ cup cooking sherry

Salt and freshly ground pepper

1 tablespoon butter

Method

Combine the fish fillet with the chicken stock in a large saucepan and poach until the fish flakes easily.

Remove the fish from the stock, chop, and set aside with the lobster and shrimp.

Add all the ingredients, except the seafood and butter, to the stock and cook for another 15 minutes.

Remove the saucepan from the heat and blend the soup in batches in an electric blender or food processor. Return the blended stock to heat, stir in the butter, and add the seafood. Cover and simmer for 5 minutes. Serve hot.

6 servings.

Hearty Cheese Soup in Sourdough Bread Bowls

A thick, creamy soup, loaded with chopped vegetables is the perfect thing to ladle into freshly baked Sourdough bread bowls.

Ingredients

5 tablespoons butter or margarine

2 medium carrots, chopped

2 stalks celery, chopped

½ cup green bell pepper, chopped

½ cup red bell pepper

1 medium onion, chopped

1 cup mushrooms, chopped

½ cup cooked ham or bacon, chopped

½ cup all-purpose flour

2 tablespoons cornstarch

4 cups chicken broth

4 cups milk

½ teaspoon paprika

¼ teaspoon cayenne pepper

½ teaspoon ground mustard

1 pound extra sharp cheddar cheese

Method

In a large, heavy stockpot, melt butter or margarine. Add chopped vegetables and ham or bacon and cook over medium heat until vegetables are slightly tender, about 10 minutes.

Stir in flour and cornstarch. Cook, stirring constantly, about three minutes. Add broth and continue stirring until slightly thickened.

Add milk and spices. Add cheese gradually, stirring until cheese is melted. To avoid curdling, do not allow soup to boil after cheese is added.

Season with salt, pepper, and serve in hallowed piping hot bread bowls. Makes 6 servings.

Neighborhood Bean Soup

Ingredients

2 cups dried great northern beans

5 cups chicken broth

3 cups water

1 large meaty ham bone

2 to 3 tablespoons chicken bouillon granules

1 teaspoon dried thyme

½ teaspoon dried marjoram

½ teaspoon pepper

¼ teaspoon rubbed sage

¼ teaspoon dried savory

2 medium onions, chopped

3 medium carrots, chopped

3 celery ribs, chopped

1 tablespoon vegetable oil

Method

1. Place beans in a Dutch oven or soup kettle; add water to cover by 2 inches. Bring to a boil; boil 2 minutes. Remove from the heat; cover and let stand for 1 hour. Drain.

2. Add broth, water, ham bone, bouillon and seasoning; bring to a boil. Reduce heat; cover and simmer for 2 hours. Sauté onions, carrots, and celery in oil; add to soup. Cover and simmer for 1 hour longer. Debone ham and cut into chunks; return to soup. Skim fat. Yield 10 servings.

Pumpkin Soup

. . . .

Ingredients

2 pounds beef, cubed

4 quarts water

2 pounds pumpkin or butternut squash, peeled and cubed

1pound potatoes, peeled and cubed

1 clove garlic

1 sprig fresh thyme or ½ teaspoon dried thyme

Salt and freshly ground pepper to taste

1 teaspoon freshly grated ginger

Method

1. Place the beef in a large soup pan, cover with the water and bring to a boil. Reduce the heat to low and simmer, uncovered until the beef is tender, about 1½ hours. Add the pumpkin, potatoes, garlic, thyme, and continue to cook until the pumpkin and potatoes are tender, about 45 minutes.

2. Remove the pumpkin and potatoes from the stock with a spoon and puree in a food processor. Return the vegetable puree to the stock. Alternately use a blender to puree the soup.

3. Season the soup with salt and pepper. Sprinkle each serving with the grated ginger; then serve.

Serves 8-10.

Red Bean Soup with Dumplings

. . . .

Ingredients

1 pound (about 2 cups) Red Kidney, Chili, or California Pink beans

1 or 2 sprigs parsley or small celery stalk with leaves

1 medium tomato, peeled, seeded and chopped

2 quarts water

½ pound pork or ham, cubed

1 teaspoon sugar

1 medium onion, finely chopped

1 ripe plantain

½ teaspoon thyme

Flour Dumplings

Method

1. In a large bowl soak beans overnight with the water. Drain the water and add pork or ham, onion, thyme, parsley, celery, tomato and sugar. Cook covered, at a simmer until the beans are tender, about 2 hours.

2. Seasoned to taste with salt and freshly ground pepper. Peel and slice the ripe plantain and add to the soup.

3. Continue cooking until the plantain is tender, and the beans have disintegrated, about half an hour. Remove the parsley and celery. Add the dumplings and cook 15 minutes longer. The beans should disintegrate to form a puree, but not a very smooth one. The soup should retain some texture. Serve 6 to 8.

Dumplings:

1 cup all-purpose flour

1 teaspoon salt

¼ cup corn meal

½ teaspoon pepper

1 teaspoon sugar

2 tablespoons unsalted butter

Sift the dry ingredients together. Rub the butter into the dry ingredients with the fingertips until the mixture is crumbly. Add enough water to make stiff dough. Form into balls about half the size of a walnut and drop into the hot bean soup. Cover and cook until the dumplings are done, about 15 minutes. Makes about 30 dumplings.

Traditionally both dumplings and plantain are added to this soup, making it almost a meal in itself. Either or both may be omitted for a lighter soup.

Southwest Chicken Soup

Ingredients

6 corn tortillas (6-inch) cut into-inch-wide strips

½ teaspoon chili powder

Pinch of salt, plus ¼ teaspoon

1 tablespoon olive oil

6 oz. boneless, skinless chicken thighs cut in ¼-inch pieces

1 small green bell pepper, chopped

1 jalapeno pepper, seeded and chopped

½ cup chopped onion

3 cloves garlic, minced

1 can (14 oz.) petite cut diced tomatoes, drained

1 can (14 oz.) low sodium vegetable broth

¼ cup water

1 teaspoon ground cumin

1 teaspoon dried oregano

¼ cup shredded cheddar cheese

2 tablespoons chopped fresh cilantro

4 lime wedges

Method

Preheat oven to 400°F.

Place tortilla strips on a baking sheet, coat with cooking spray, and sprinkle with chili powder and pinch of salt. Bake until crisp, about 6 to 8 minutes.

Meanwhile, heat oil in a medium saucepan over medium heat. Sauté chicken thigh pieces until lightly browned, 1 to 2 minutes. Add bell pepper, jalapeño pepper, onion, and garlic, and cook until onions are tender, 2 to 3 minutes. Stir in tomatoes and cook 1 minute.

Add broth, water, cumin, oregano, and remaining ¼ teaspoon salt to pan and bring to a boil over high heat. Divide soup among bowls and top with tortilla strips, cheese, and cilantro. Serve with lime wedges for squeezing.

TIP: The chile-flavored baked corn tortilla strips make this soup especially good. But in a pinch, you could substitute store-bought tortilla chips.

Vegetables

Baked Squash With Apples

Ingredients

2 pounds butternut squash

4 baking apples cored and peeled

½ cup brown sugar

¼ cup margarine, melted

1 tablespoon flour

1 teaspoon salt

1 teaspoon cinnamon

dash of cloves

Method

Cut each squash in half. Remove seeds and fiber. Peel and cut into ½ inch slices. Arrange squash in ungreased oblong pan. Top with apple slices evenly over squash. Mix brown sugar, margarine, flour, salt, cinnamon, nutmeg and cloves. Sprinkle over top. If desired top with ½ cup walnuts. Cover loosely with foil and bake at 350° F for 60 minutes or until tender.

Brown Rice Slaw

. . . .

Ingredients

2 cups coleslaw mix

2 cups cooked brown rice

1 medium tart apple, chopped

1/3 cup orange juice concentrate

1/3 cup fat free mayonnaise

1 teaspoon sugar

¼ teaspoon salt

¼ cup chopped pecans, toasted

Method

In a bowl, combine the coleslaw mix, rice and apple. In a small bowl, combine orange juice concentrate, mayonnaise, sugar and salt; pour over coleslaw mixture and toss to coat. Cover and refrigerate until serving. Stir in pecans. Makes 8 servings.

Fried Green Tomatoes

. . . .

Ingredients

3 full sized green tomatoes

½ cup cornmeal

¾ teaspoon salt

¾ teaspoon ground black pepper

1 teaspoon paprika

1 teaspoon all purpose flour

3 tablespoons vegetable oil

Method

Core the tomatoes and then cut them crosswise into thick slices. In a shallow bowl, combine the cornmeal, pepper, paprika, and flour. Dredge the tomato slices in the cornmeal mixture and set in single layer on a plate. You will not use all of the coating; reserve the remainder. Put the plate in the freezer for 5 minutes to allow the moisture from the tomatoes to soak up the coating.

In a nonstick skillet over medium high heat, warm the oil. Remove the tomatoes from the freezer and dredge in the remaining cornmeal mixture. Fry the tomatoes, turning once, until browned on both sides, about 3 minutes on each side. Serve hot. Serves 6.

Green Bean Casserole

Ingredients

1 can (18 oz.) creamy mushroom soup

1 teaspoon soy sauce

Dash ground black pepper

2 tablespoons plain breadcrumbs

3 cans (14.5 oz. each) cut green beans, drained

1 can (2.8 oz.) French fried onions

Method

Heat oven to 350°F. In an ungreased 1½ quart casserole, mix soup, soy sauce, pepper, breadcrumbs, green beans and 2/3 cup of the onions.

Bake about 30 minutes or until hot and bubbly. Stir; sprinkle with remaining onions.

Bake about 10 minutes longer or until onions are golden brown.

Yield: 6 servings.

Green Bean Parmesan

. . . .

Ingredients

2 9-oz. packages frozen French style green beans

1¼ milk

¼ cup chopped onion

2 teaspoons butter or margarine

2 tablespoons all-purpose flour

½ teaspoon salt

¼ cup grated Parmesan cheese

1 5-oz. can water chestnuts, drained and sliced

¾ cup soft breadcrumbs

2 teaspoons butter, melted

Method

1. Cook beans according to package directions; drain, reserving liquid. Add milk to reserved liquid to make 1¼ cup; set aside.

2. In a saucepan cook onion in 2 tablespoons butter till tender; blend in flour and salt.

3. Stir in milk mixture all at once; cook and stir till thickened and bubbly.

4. Stir in half the Parmesan cheese. Stir in the cooked beans and sliced water chestnuts; place in a 1 quart casserole.

5. Toss crumbs with remaining Parmesan and melted butter to combine; sprinkle atop casserole. Bake uncovered at 350° degrees till bubbly for about 30 minutes. Garnish with additional sliced water chestnuts, if desired. Makes 6 to 8 servings.

Instant Potatoes

Ingredients

Starting with a mix
Mashed Potato Stir-Ins

Method

Prepare instant mashed potato puffs as directed on package for 4 servings. Just before serving, try one of the following additions:

- **Bacon:** Stir in 1 to 2 slices bacon, crisply fried and crumbled.
- **Blue Cheese:** Stir in 1 to 1½ tablespoons crumbled blue cheese.
- **Celery Seed:** Stir in ½ teaspoon celery seed.
- **Chives:** Stir in 1 tablespoon snipped chives
- **Dill:** Stir in ¼ teaspoon dill weed.
- **Green Pepper:** Stir in 1 tablespoon chopped green pepper.
- **Mushroom:** Stir in 1 can (2 ounces) mushroom stems and pieces, drained.
- **Mustard:** Stir in 1½ teaspoon prepared mustard.
- **Olive:** Stir in 1½ teaspoons sliced pitted ripe olives or 1½ tablespoons sliced pimento-stuffed olives.
- **Pimento:** Stir in 1 tablespoon chopped drained pimiento.

Orange Glazed Sweet Potatoes

Ingredients

2 pounds sweet potatoes

6 tablespoons butter

1/3 cup brown sugar

¼ cup maple syrup

½ teaspoon orange peel

¾ cup orange juice

1 tablespoon cornstarch

½ teaspoon ground cinnamon

¼ teaspoon ground nutmeg

Topping

1/3 old fashioned oats

¼ cup brown sugar

½ teaspoon ground cinnamon

2 tablespoons butter

Method

Cook sweet potatoes in boiling water for 20 minutes on medium heat. Arrange potatoes in a 2 quart buttered shallow baking dish with slices overlapped.

In a saucepan, combine sugar, orange juice, orange peel, maple syrup, butter, cornstarch and bring to a boil over high heat until it thickened for 5 minutes. Pour over potatoes.

In a small bowl, combine oats, sugar and cinnamon. Cut in butter until crumbly. Sprinkle over potatoes. Bake, uncovered, at 350° for 30 minutes.

Yield: 8 servings.

Stir Fry Chinese Cabbage

Ingredients

2 teaspoon olive oil

2 teaspoons minced garlic

½ head Chinese cabbage, cleaned and sliced

1 small zucchini, sliced

½ green bell pepper

½ red bell pepper

2 teaspoon soy sauce

1 teaspoon rice vinegar

1 teaspoon cayenne pepper

2 teaspoon toasted sesame oil

1 small onion diced

1 teaspoon dry thyme

Salt to taste

Method

In a large pan over medium heat, add 2 teaspoons olive oil, 2 teaspoons minced garlic and sauté, stirring for about 1 minute. Add the Chinese cabbage, zucchini, green bell pepper, red bell pepper and cook until just starting to wilt, about 3 minutes. Add soy sauce, rice vinegar, cayenne pepper, and thyme, salt and stir well and cook just until cabbage is wilted. Add chopped onion and stir into pan and cook for 2 minutes. Remove from heat and add sesame oil.

Yield 6 servings.

Vegetable and Garbanzo Curry

. . . .

Ingredients

3 cups cauliflower florets

1 15-oz. can garbanzo beans (chickpea),
rinsed and drained

1 cup frozen cut green beans

1 cup sliced carrots

½ cup chopped onion

1 14-oz. can vegetable broth

2 to 3 teaspoons curry powder

1 14-oz. can light coconut milk

¼ cup shredded fresh basil leaves

Method

1. In a 3 ½ or 4 quart slow cooker, combine cauliflower, garbanzo beans, green beans, carrot, and onion. Stir in broth and curry powder.

2. Cover and cook on low heat setting for 5 to 6 hours or on high heat setting for 2 ½ to 3 hours. Stir in coconut milk and basil leaves. Makes 4 to 6 servings.

Zucchini in Batter

Ingredients

1 cup water

2/3 cup flour

2 zucchini squash cut in slices

Vegetable oil for frying

Salt to taste

Method

1. Put 1 cup water in a bowl and gradually add 2/3 cup flour, beat mixture until smooth.
2. Dip ¼ inch slices of zucchini in batter and brown in an inch of vegetable oil.
3. Turn once to brown on second side. Drain and add a little salt and pepper.
4. Repeat step 2 and 3 until finished.

COOKING TERMS

Au gratin: Topped with crumbs and or cheese and browned in oven or under broiler.

Au jus: Served in its own juices.

Baste: To moisten foods during cooking with pan drippings or special sauce in order to add flavor and prevent drying.

Bisque: A thick cream soup.

Blanch: To immense in rapidly boiling water and allow to cook slightly.

Cream: To soften a fat, especially butter, by beating it at room temperature. Butter and sugar are often creamed together, making a smooth soft paste.

Crimp: To seal the edges of a two-crust pie either by pinching them at intervals with the fingers or by pressing them together with the tip of a folk.

Degrease: To remove fat from surfaces of stews, soups or stock. Usually cooled in the refrigerator so that fat hardens and is easily removed.

Dredge: To coat lightly with flour, cornmeal, etc.

Entrée: The main course.

Fold: To incorporate a delicate substance, such as whipped cream or beaten egg whites, into another substance without releasing air bubbles. A spatula is used to gently bring part of the mixture from the bottom of the bowl to the top. The process is repeated, while slowly rotating the bowl, until the ingredients are thoroughly blended.

Glaze: To cover with a glossy coating, such as a melted and somewhat diluted jelly for fruit desserts.

Julienne: To cut or slice vegetables, fruits or cheeses into match-shaped slivers.

Marinate: To allow food to stand in liquid in order to tenderize or to add flavor.

Mince: To chop food into very small pieces.

Parboil: To boil until partially cooked; to blanch. Usually final cooking in a seasoned sauce follows this procedure.

Pare: To remove the outermost skin of a fruit or vegetable.

Puree: To mash foods by hand by rubbing through a sieve or food mill, or by whirling in a blender or food processor until perfectly smooth.

Refresh: To run cold water over food that has been parboiled in order to stop the cooking process quickly.

Saute: To cook and/or brown food in a small quantity of hot shortening.

Scald: To heat to just below the boiling point, when tiny bubbles appears at the edge of the saucepan.

Simmer: To cook in liquid just below the boiling point. The surface of the liquid should be barely moving, broken from time to time by slowly rising bubbles.

Steep: To let food stand in hot liquid in order to extract or to enhance flavor, like tea in hot water or poached fruit in syrup.

Toss: To combine ingredients with a repeated lifting motion.

Whip: To beat rapidly in order to incorporate air and produce expansion, as in heavy cream or egg whites.

TROPICAL INGREDIENTS GLOSSARY

Ackee (akee) - The ackee is found throughout the Caribbean, and is the national fruit in Jamaica. It originally derived from West Africa is cooked with salted fish to make that country's national dish. Ackee is a triangular fruit with a red coat. When ripe, ackee splits in three while the yellowish edible portion part is cooked fresh.

Arrowroot - starch is used to thicken pudding, sauces and glazes. Arrowroot is available in health food stores, specialty food stores, and some supermarkets.

Avocado - They are green and usually sold unripe and are hard to touch. When ripe, it can be used by itself, in salads, and guacamole. Avocado is grown commercially throughout the tropical America and the islands of the Caribbean.

Banana *(banane)* - This fruit comes in both green and ripe and are used in Caribbean cooking. They are prepared whole, mashed, creamed and fried. Bananas can be used as a substitute for plantain. Can be eaten ripe and can be cooked when green for 20 minutes. To cook green bananas, take a knife, peel the bananas and then can be boiled in hot salted water. Their flesh is firm and starchy like boiled potatoes. Bananas are high in vitamins and are well known in the Caribbean. This fruit is loaded with potassium. Can be eaten as a starch when it is green.

Breadfruit - is a large green fruit that comes in different sizes. Breadfruit has bumpy skin. It can be boiled like potato, roasted in the skin especially in a coal-pot, then peeled, fried, or eat with fish or any meat stew.

Callaloo - A green leafy vegetable that looks like Chinese spinach. Callaloo is widely grown in Jamaica. It is used in soups or served as a vegetable side dish. The vegetable is available fresh or canned in the West Indian food stores.

Cashew – An evergreen tree and shrub a native to the West Indies. It bears a reddish or yellow pear-shaped cashew apple from the bottom, which grows a kidney shaped nut. The pear is edible only when ripe. The nut is eaten only when roasted.

Cassava (manioc) - a root vegetable used as an addition to soups and meat dishes. Tapioca comes from the cassava. It is available in Hispanic grocery stores. Cassava is a woody shrub that is cultivated as an annual crop in tropical regions. Cassava root is very rich in starch.

Chili Peppers - Hot chili peppers are frequently used in the Caribbean islands cooking. Sometimes they are available in supermarkets that import foods. The peppers may be red, green, or yellow and comes in different sizes. If your recipe asks for chili peppers, remove the seeds first before adding to your dish. Wash your hands after handling hot peppers as this may get into your eyes or play it safe by using gloves.

Chive - (Chives) can be either fresh or dried herb with a slight onion flavor and used in a variety of fish, meat and vegetable dishes.

Cho-cho - is an edible Caribbean vegetable that is also known as Christophene, Chayote, vegetable pear, mirliton, and mango squash. Trinidadians use it as a vegetable too. It can be sliced and added to Chow Mein noodles. Cho-cho is also a plant that belongs to the gourd family.

Christophene - A light green pear shape with grooves. This vegetable is grown in Central and South America and tropical countries. Has rough skin and ribs running lengthwise and trimmed with prickles. This vegetable can be pureed, baked, creamed, or steamed. In the Caribbean, people slice and cook with meat or salted fish.

Coconut - Coconut is grown in tropical countries and certain parts of the tropics on a 50 to 80 feet palm tree that provides young green nuts of various sizes. The coconut tree can produce 50 coconuts in one crop. When mature enough, the color changes to brown. Afterwards the palm around the nuts starts to fall to the ground then the coconuts also starts to fall later. To open the coconut, place the coconut facing the ground and cut/hit with a machete or a cutlass to remove the heavy fibrous husk. Take the meat out of the shell with a knife.

Coconut water - is an excellent thirst quencher when the temperature is humid in the Caribbean islands. Vendors sell coconut on the streets to merchants and tourists. The young coconut has an edible meat inside which is not too sweet. If you try eating one coconut, you will find the meat inside can decrease your hunger too. Coconuts produce thick meat that most people eat after drinking its water. When properly matured, many people eat the meat that is about ½ inch thick inside the nut itself.

Coconut Milk or cream is extracted from the hard meat of a coconut. Most people use it's milk for various food preparations such as appetizers, pastries, oil. Grate the coconut meat to make the milk. Measure the coconut and add an equal amount of hot water. Cover bowl with a piece of cloth and strain the coconut through the cloth, pressing down hard on the coconut. If you measure 1½ cups of coconut meat to 1½ cups of water, you should produce 1½ cups of coconut milk.

Cointreau - The bitter oranges used to give its unique flavor are found in Haiti, Spain, and Brazil.

Conch (lambi Concha) - Conch is eaten raw in salads, cooked in soups, stews, and fritters in all Caribbean islands. Is available in large fish markets in the United States. For best results, conch should be cut in small pieces for easier handling.

Dasheen (tannia) The young dasheen shoots and leaves are used just like spinach. It is available in West Indian food markets. These leaves are used in soups and meats.

Eggplant - egg-shaped vegetable having a shiny skin typically dark purple but occasionally white or yellow. Eggplant is a hairy upright herb native to southeastern Asia but widely cultivated for its large glossy edible fruit commonly used as a vegetable.

Fennel Seed - is a highly aromatic and flavorful herb with culinary and medicinal uses, and is one of the primary ingredients or substitute of anise and other aromatics.

Ginger - is a plant that is consumed whole as a delicacy, medicine, or spice. It lends its name to its genus and family. Other notable members of this plant family are turmeric and cardamom. Ginger cultivation began in South Asia and has since spread to East Africa and the Caribbean. It is sometimes called root ginger to distinguish it from other things that share the name ginger

Golden Apple - The flesh of a golden apple fruit can be squeezed to produce an acidic juice. The juice of golden apple fruit is also used as a component of multi-fruit juices, as it can be too bitter to be consumed by itself. It is hard and green at first but grows soft and yellow upon ripening, hence its nickname "golden apple" fruit. Its flavor and scent are similar to those of pineapple.

Guava – The flesh of this plum size fruit is pink and has seeds inside. It has green or yellow skin and is edible. Jellies, beverages and sherbets can be made from this fruit. When ripe, a juicy guava can be eaten with the fingers.

Kahlua Coffee – A coffee liqueur produced in Mexico with 26 percent alcohol by volume. Kahlua is the world's most popular and versatile liqueur often noted as a top 20 spirit across the US. Though its popularity originated in hot drinks and food recipes, there are now hundred of drink recipes made with kahlua.

Madere – Tuber whose hearty leaves and stalks are also eaten; called "dachine" in Martinique, St. Lucia, and Madere in Guadeloupe.

Mango - is a yellowish red tropical fruit with a firm skin, hard central stone, and juicy aromatic sub-acid pulp. Mangos basically require a frost-free climate. Flowers and small fruit can be killed if temperatures drop below 40°F, even for a short period. There are many varieties of mangoes, usually distinguishable by shape and the consistency of the flesh. Eaten ripe, the fruit is aromatic, and the flesh is soft and sweet. Mango is also used to make nectar and ice-cream.

Masala – Roasted and ground spice mix, including cinnamon, cumin, nutmeg, and cardamom.

Mascarpone Cheese - An Italian cream cheese.

Okras – Also known as gumbo. This plant produces pod-like fruits. Each pod is oblong in shape and pointed at one end with a soft sticky interior. The pod is cooked as a vegetable.

Orange Liqueur – A strongly flavored sweet liquor or cordial usually drank after a meal. It is flavored with sour orange peel, triple sec. This type of curacoa have a higher alcoholic content.

Papaya (papaw) - A papaw is ripe when yellow. Ripe papaws can be used in beverages, ice creams, and sherbets, or eaten plain like watermelon. Papaws are widely available in produce section of supermarkets.

Passion Fruit - The flavorful translucent sop is scooped out of the hollow husks of the passion fruit for a delightful taste experience. Passion fruit juice is a preferred thirst quencher.

Pigeon Peas - Fresh pigeon peas are green. Dried peas are soaked overnight. They are cooked with soups or with rice. Can be purchased in canned or fresh.

Pineapple - This popular fruit is a native of Central and South America and was introduced to the West Indies by the Spanish who also took the plant to Europe. Pineapples can be eaten or crushed to make juice. The fruit is as an ingredient or garnish in many cocktails.

Plantain – is larger than the regular banana. A ripe plantain can be fried, boiled, or mashed. A ripe plantain can turn black if stored in the refrigerator. Should not be eaten raw. When used unripe, it must be boiled as it becomes hard when it's cold. Slit the fruit lengthwise to get to the plantain either ripe or unripe. When cooked green, plantain is treated like boiled potatoes and can be eaten with any stewed meat. Green or ripe plantain can be added to soup by removing the skin.

Pumpkin – The Caribbean pumpkin is round or oval in shape. It has green skin with bright yellowish flesh and is used in soups, or served mashed. Caribbean pumpkin is available in West Indian food markets.

Red Snapper – Red snapper has a lean but firm flesh with a distinctive flavor. If not available, substitute with any white firm fleshed fish such as perch, haddock, sea bass, grouper or sole.

Salt Beef – Salt beef can be found in specialty food stores that carry Caribbean foods. It is stewed beef that has been preserved with either dry salt or brine. This was the only method available to preserve the meat.

Salt Fish – Salt Fish is available in some supermarkets in Caribbean countries and also in the United States. It can be purchased with or without bones. Before using salt fish, soak the fish in cold water several hours or even overnight to remove the majority of the salt. If you do not have time to soak the fish for several hours, simply put the fish in a saucepan of cold water to boil. Afterwards, drain the salted water and add more cold water to remove the salt. To determine how much salt is left in the

fish, you must taste. When desalted, flake it with a folk.

Scotch Bonnet Chili – Small and extremely hot lantern-shape chili, it comes in a range of colors, from light green to red.

Sea Breams - are sought after because of their mild, white meat, considered some of the best of any white-meat fish.

Smoked Herring - (Is used especially as meats and fish) dried and cured by hanging in wood smoke.

Sorrel – This is a tropical plant. They are available fresh and dried in health food stores and West Indian food shops. Sorrel is a plant with roots that run deep into the ground. The sepals are removed and used fresh or dried in beverages and jellies but are packaged at health food stores.

Soursop (corossol) – A dark green fruit with white flesh and a tart taste. It is used in beverages, ice cream, and sherbets. It is difficult to locate fresh sweetsop outside of the Caribbean, but can be found as soursop nectar at some supermarkets in the United States.

Sweet Potato – This starchy root vegetable can be baked or mashed. This potato has a reddish or brownish skin and can be found mostly in Asian supermarkets or West Indian food stores.

Tamarind – This is a fruit tree grown in the tropics. The fruit has an acidic pulp inside where the hidden seeds are covered. The pulp is sour, and sugar can be added to the seeds to make candies and beverages. This fruit is often sold pressed into compact blocks and it is used as a condiment. This can be purchased at West Indian stores.

Tannia – tropical vegetable having edible tubers that are cooked and eaten like yams or potatoes. Can be found in supermarkets in US.

Triple Sec is a liqueur that is sweet in flavor, although it is not overly so. It lends sweetness and a hint of orange flavor to many mixed drink recipes.

Watermelon - A relative of the cantaloupe, the watermelon provides an overwhelmingly juicy mouthful with every bite. The fruit is also blended into a refreshing drink.

Yams – Yams vary in size, shape, and texture. Caribbean yams can be white, yellow, waxy, dry, or hard. They can be bland and sweet. Yams can be cooked in soups, and served as a side dish, mashed, baked or boiled. They are not the sweet potato used for Thanksgiving or Christmas dishes.

ALPHABETICAL SEQUENCE
TABLE OF
CONTENTS

A

B

C

G

H

P

Q

R

T

V

W

Z